The Five-Minute Rule

The Story of
a Seeker, a Sage,
and the Secret to a Happy Life

Danny
We all can "M
a difference

Rory

Rory J. Aplanalp and Donald P. Mangum

Jacket Art and illustrations by Mona Hennes

Jacket Design by Cindy Aplanalp – Houston, Texas

Printed by Specialty Bindery and Printing – Houston, Texas

©Rory J Aplanalp and Donald P Mangum

All rights reserved. No part of this book may be reproduced in any form or by any means without express permission in writing from the publisher, Starlight Publishing, 2425 West Loop South, Suite 200, Houston, Texas 77068. The story presented herein is solely from the imagination of the authors, and they alone take full responsibility for any of its contents.

First Printing August 2003

Library of Congress Cataloging-in-Publication Data

Aplanalp, Rory J., 1951
    The Five-Minute Rule

    1.   Mangum, Donald P.

ISBN 0-9743330-1-8

Printed in the United States of America

10 9 8 7 6 5 4 3 2 1

Contents

ACKNOWLEDGMENTS

Most books are written with the help of many people besides the authors. In many respects this writing effort has been a team effort or collaboration. Because of that, we wish to thank those who helped us along the way.

Donald Mangum, Jr., and our wives, Cindy Aplanalp and Diane Mangum, participated with us in many long discussions as the book unfolded. Their ideas, suggestions and creative input added much to the content. We deeply appreciate their patience and understanding as we all wrestled with the best ways to express ideas.

Because the content of this book centers on principles of living, we are deeply grateful to those who have most influenced the development of those principles in our own lives. Rory's parents, Arden and Marie Dean Aplanalp, and Don's parents, James and Ethlene Mangum provided the foundation. Our wives, Cindy and Diane, continued the process, and our children have added much to our understanding. To all of them we express heartfelt appreciation.

We are also deeply grateful for the able efforts of our editors, Linda Martin, Lisa Crockett and Adam Mangum. Each one added much to the contents of this book and did their best to help us steer a course of clarity and good expression.

FOREWORD

The authors met about twenty years ago in Salt Lake City, Utah. At the time, they were both young professionals helping raise young families. Gradually, a friendship blossomed. Job transfers eventually resulted in cross-country moves for both—Rory to Houston, Texas, and Don to Boston, Massachusetts. Due to the distance and intense professional demands, they lost contact with each other. In the summer of 2002, Don and his family moved to Houston, resulting in a renewed friendship between the authors. Late one night a few months later, the idea of this book was born in their collective imaginations.

Rory's years of keynote speaking, his master storytelling skills, and his strong desire to "make a difference" had resulted in a presentation designed to help others make better use of their time in this helter-skelter world. And Don's corporate training background, his own storytelling skills mixed with a vivid imagination and previous writing experiences, made a good match for the creation of this book.

What follows is a fictional presentation of very practical ideas. Many of the anecdotes you will read are based on real life experiences of the authors. They are, in fact, true but may have been altered slightly to fit into the story or to protect the privacy of others.

We hope you enjoy *The Five-Minute Rule*.

The Publishers

1

The Odyssey Begins

It couldn't be a blizzard this late in March, thought the young man, but it seemed like one to him as he made his way across the snow encrusted lawn, pushing himself hard against the icy, howling wind. It was dark, it was cold, and he wasn't sure he wanted to be there. But he didn't have anywhere else to go. On one of the bleakest days of his life, he needed to talk with someone who wouldn't just tell him he'd made some serious mistakes. He already knew that. What he needed was a friend, someone who would give him hope, but also someone wise enough to help him set a new course. Reaching the porch, he carefully ascended the stairs and while huddling against the wall of the enclosed entryway, he pushed the doorbell.

When the door opened, the young man was relieved to see his friend standing in front of him. At least he wouldn't have to make small talk with a member of the family. The older man was puzzled at first as he squinted into the faint illumination of the porch light. Then, recognizing the visitor, he quickly invited him in. "What on earth brings you out on a night like this?" he asked, while taking a snow-covered coat and hanging it in the hall closet.

"Is there somewhere we can talk privately?" was the almost whispered response.

"Of course," responded the older man, "let's go to my study."

After they were settled comfortably, the young man began speaking. First, a trickle of hesitant conversation; then a gentle stream, filled with halting, cautious sentences; finally a flood of words and tears. The story was simultaneously familiar and unique to the host. The young man's early years had been like most boys his age in the community—school, friends, sports, and church. Then shortly after high school, he served as a full-time volunteer for his church in South America. Two years later, the young man, many rich spiritual experiences behind him, returned home to his proud family. Life was great. College days, dating, courtship and marriage followed in rapid succession. Soon children arrived, professional work began, and life got even better.

Then a small crack appeared in the protective shell of his basic values. The crack occurred in a very short period of time, perhaps only five minutes or so. But into the crack seeped influences, ideas, thoughts, and desires that were unfamiliar but tantalizing. Curiosity quickly overturned wisdom, and the unfamiliar became more intriguing, even exciting. Living close to the edge was a thrill. And the dark influences, which first came slowly into a small opening, soon broke through, shattering the young man's resolve.

And the results of such choices and behavior? Broken promises to his wife and small children, disaffection from the religion of his youth, followed by tears, separation, and divorce. "Life is great" was replaced with humiliation and sorrow, followed by poignant questions. Will God forgive me? Can I recover? Can I ever repair the damage I've caused or do anything of value in the lives of others?

And now, after almost a year of struggling with these questions, the young man had come seeking answers from

2

an old family friend, a man widely known for his wisdom in helping others resolve difficult problems, someone he had known since childhood. The friend did not respond with platitudes or clichés. In fact, he spoke very little, but listened intently.

"You have presented some very difficult issues," the host began, when the young man finished his story. "Like you, many have come to this house searching for help; some have made unwise or foolish choices, some have been victims of the tragic choices of others, and some have suffered extraordinary pain from the ebb and flow of their lives. They've come seeking answers to almost imponderable questions like those you've asked tonight, or even more difficult ones. Why me? Why now? What did I do to deserve this? Why such pain for an innocent child? There are no good answers for such questions. Experience has taught me that altering the course of one's life is no simple matter, nor is the altering of one's perception of the meaning of events to be achieved easily.

"However, the fact that you are here tells me you are about to begin a long and challenging odyssey. By experience I know that those who persist on such journeys eventually find what they're seeking. The answers to your questions don't come easily, but they can be found. It feels like you're ready to embark. As you do, I suggest that you keep a journal, a record of your feelings, your thoughts, and your experiences along the way. If you don't already have one, perhaps you could purchase a journal before we meet again."

An appointment was set and the young man left, re-entering the howling storm bundled in a wool coat, fleece-lined gloves, and a hat that could be pulled down over his ears. He needed them all.

Several evenings later, the young man came again to the home of his friend, having suffered through long and difficult days as he continued to wrestle with his feelings about the tragic effects of his choices. The snow was still present, though it was now piled high around the walkways. A brisk chill was in the air. The visitor was greeted warmly and was soon sitting in the study with his friend.

After a few minutes of conversation, the host asked the young man about his week and what he had done with his time. He also asked about his thoughts and feelings since their last meeting. The guest talked about the ongoing struggle with sense of self-worth. He said he was doubtful he could recover personally or repair the damage caused by his ill-fated choices. The older man listened to the answers with little interruption, nodding occasionally and asking relevant questions. He said very few words the young man could hold onto in his quest to gain peace of mind. Instead, he took an unexpected approach. When he was certain that the narrative was finished, the older man reached into a drawer of his desk. "I have a gift for you," he said kindly, handing a handsomely-wrapped package to the young man. "Perhaps it will help you gain perspective."

Curious, the visitor opened the gift. Inside, he found an hourglass set in a dark cherry wood frame. He carefully lifted it out of the box and placed it on the table between them. It was the height of two hands placed one on top of the other. And as would be expected, all the sand was in the bottom. Puzzled, the young man looked quizzically at his host.

"Turn it over and tell me what you see," suggested the friend.

As he did so, the sand began to flow ever so slowly into the empty space. The young man described the process, "I see sand pulled by gravity through a small hole, falling into the bottom and gradually filling it."

"That's good for a start," the friend answered.

Then in a moment of understanding, the young man asked, "What do *you* see?"

"What do I see? In this hourglass I see part of the answer to the three vital questions you asked last week," the host responded. Then continuing, he added, "I have an assignment for you. Take the hourglass, study it, and when you think you see what I see, call me and we'll talk again."

Several weeks passed and the young man studied the hourglass for a few minutes each day. Finally, in frustration, he called his friend and told him he needed help with the assignment.

That evening, in the solitude of the study, the two men sat at the table, looking at the hourglass. "Tell me what you see," the host asked pleasantly.

"I see individual grains of sand falling relentlessly through a narrow hole," the young man began. "I also see that this is an unusual hourglass, as only a single grain can pass through it at a time. And I see that when the hourglass is working, the sand represents three dimensions of time— past, present, and future. The future is the sand in the top, the present is a single grain as it passes through the opening, and the past is all the sand collecting in the bottom. What I do not see is how this represents an answer to my three questions."

"You're making great progress," his host responded in a tone that suggested both excitement and encouragement. "Not everyone sees the three dimensions of time this quickly. If you continue to examine the hourglass, you'll find other keys that will help you in your quest. For example, think about the individual grains as they pass through the narrow opening. Consider why they might be important."

The young man was listening carefully, but they both knew that he was not ready to answer any more questions. So his host changed his approach. "Was there anything else that occurred to you while you studied the hourglass?"

After a brief reflection, the young man offered, "Yes, there was one other curious thing. I even wrote it down. The simple activity of pondering the meaning of time has brought a sense of peace to me, and I'm not sure why."

"That's a good observation. You'll want to give that more thought. I'm also pleased to see that you are using your journal regularly. It's a very useful tool." The host reached over to his desk to pick up another wrapped box. "I have something else to give you, and I think you're ready for it tonight." Sliding the package across the table, he suggested the young man open it at home.

"I'll bet it's another mystery." He smiled as he accepted the gift.

"So it is," his friend responded kindly. "A more challenging one, I think. But this is all the time I have tonight. After you've examined the second gift, call me. You'll also want to continue studying the hourglass. You're on the right track there."

The young man eagerly returned to his apartment. Tossing his coat aside, he quickly unwrapped the new gift at the kitchen table. Inside he found a hand mirror ornately decorated with expensive jewels embedded in the crystal frame. The frame extended into a long handle. The back was of polished brass, and the entire mirror had the appearance of a very expensive work of art, created a long time ago. The young man thought of the Socratic approach of his mentor and amused himself by asking the obvious question.

"Tell me what you see," he said out loud, trying to mimic his friend's approach. "But take your time."

Slowly the young man examined the mirror. He found himself staring at his reflection, trying to understand if this was what he was supposed to see. He carefully examined the workmanship and wondered if there was an answer in the value of the jewel-encrusted mirror.

While looking at the mirror, he answered his friend's imagined question. "I see myself framed in an expensive crystal mirror. I see more than myself, because when I look carefully at the reflection, I see things in the background. This one is a puzzle." Then noting the lateness of the hour, he concluded his search with the thought, "At least I'll have something to think about as I fall asleep."

He thought about the mirror all the next day while he was at work, considering a multitude of possibilities of its significance: What you see is what you get, seeing is believing, take time for reflection, and many other ideas that he eventually tossed aside as being too simplistic. He was almost too preoccupied to focus on his sales calls, but the day went fast.

Immediately after supper, in the early evening with sunlight quickly fading, he picked up the mirror again and looked at his reflection. Remembering his friend's remark that this mystery would be more difficult to solve than the hourglass, he decided to examine the whole object and not assume that the answer was in his own reflection. He turned it over and looked carefully at the back for the first time. As he moved his fingers across the polished brass surface, he could feel almost invisible markings in the metal. He concluded that it was an old engraving, almost worn away. In his hurry, he hadn't really noticed it before. Taking a piece of paper and holding it carefully against the metal, he rubbed a pencil gently on the paper. Gradually two faint lines of text appeared:

What you see

Is not all of me

"I don't know if the message helps or not," he said out loud. Later, he went to bed still thinking about the words. The next day was Saturday. As soon as he awoke, he hurried to the table and picked up the mirror. Briefly touching the polished back to remind him of the message, he looked deeply into his reflection and thought again of the words "What you see is not all of me."

"So that's it," he asserted, triumphantly. "The message is about me, myself, not about the mirror! At least that's progress. But, I'll need to think about this *and* the hourglass for few more days."

The following Wednesday morning, he called his friend and arranged to see him that night. Soon they were in the study. This time the young man was visibly excited.

"I've solved part of the riddle of the mirror, but I don't have it all, yet."

"Tell me what you've discovered," the friend encouraged.

"I found the old engravings," he answered enthusiastically, "and I've been thinking about the words, *'What you see is not all of me.'* There are endless possibilities for what it means."

"You've been a good detective," the host observed. "Tell me one of your ideas."

"Well, first of all the message is about me, not the mirror," he answered slowly. "And one possible meaning is that when I'm out in public, people can only see my behavior, what's on the outside. They cannot see my desires or my motives, which are frequently far more important than what I do. This suggests that I need to have integrity in my actions, making them a true reflection of what can't be seen. I haven't always been that way in the past."

"Few of us always are. But we can get better at it," his host observed. "That's a great start. What else did you notice about the mirror?"

"I think the exquisite beauty of the mirror is a distraction from the real message, much like material things are often a distraction from the real purposes of life. So that's where I am now."

"As you can see, each gift may have more than one meaning or use," said the host. "I think you'll eventually discover how to use the gifts to guide you to truth. You're certainly well on your way. Have you discovered anything new about the hourglass?"

"I've been thinking a lot about the grain of sand as it passes through the small opening in the hourglass," the visitor answered confidently. "It represents the present and highlights the importance of the present moment, which passes so rapidly before us. I think I'm getting closer to unlocking the mystery."

"You are, but as you've implied, you're far from finished," his host stated with a tone that suggested helpfulness. "And now, I have another gift. It comes in several parts. Stepping to his bookshelf, the friend reached for two packages, one large and one smaller. Pushing the larger package across the table, he asked the young man to open it.

When the wrapping paper was pulled aside, a stunning mahogany box was uncovered. It was rectangular in shape and reminded the young man of a costly jewelry box. With a nod of silent encouragement from his host, he raised the lid until it stayed open on its own. Looking inside with eager anticipation of both the content and the coming question, he whispered, "It's empty. The inside is covered with felt, but I don't see anything else."

"It's not empty."

Immediately the guest moved his fingers all along the dark maroon covering, but finding no hidden articles or compartments, he repeated his assertion. "It *is* empty. There's nothing in it."

"My friend, it only appears empty," the host insisted. "But it will take a little time to find what's there. I have another package that will help you."

He handed a large envelope to the young man and asked him to open it. Inside were four smaller, numbered envelopes and a set of simple instructions. "Open the envelopes now, and read the instructions for each. Complete the assignment for envelope number one before proceeding to number two, and so forth."

Reaching for envelope number one, he found it unsealed. On the outside of this envelope was an address. Inside were a key and a piece of paper with these instructions: "Drive to the address, park in front, then walk along the left side of the building until you come to a door. Use the key to enter. Once inside, determine what's in the room."

In envelope number two were directions to the city park and these instructions: "Within the next few weeks, drive to the park on a clear, sunny Saturday, arriving at exactly 10:00 AM. After parking in the lot beside the highway, walk along the sidewalk until you come to a 'Y.' Sit on the bench you find there. Look around. What's in the park? When you're satisfied with your answer, think about the meaning of the mirror."

The third envelope contained a map giving directions to a property several miles away. A key was included with a typewritten note: "When you arrive at the property, use the enclosed key to unlock the wrought iron gate that crosses the road. After you drive onto the property, close the gate and lock it. Continue driving to the end of the road. Park and follow the path on your right until you come to a meadow. It's only a minute or two away. Take a blanket, spread it out in a comfortable place, and sit down. After you've allowed yourself to relax, answer this question: What do you feel?"

The fourth envelope contained yet another note with these instructions: "After you've visited these three locations, open the box again and see what's in it. When you've completed your assignments, and can solve this last riddle, call me to arrange another appointment."

Time passed quickly for the young man. He visited all the suggested locations. After the final journey, he returned to his apartment, opened his journal, and reviewed the conclusions he had drawn from each experience. He also examined the box, seeking to understand both what was in the box and what significance it had for him. He studied the mirror and the hourglass again. When he thought he was ready, he called his friend.

A day later, he was ushered into the now-familiar study. He looked neither excited nor discouraged. As they sat down on the opposite couches, the young man placed all the gifts on the table between them.

"What's in the box?" the host asked.

"Space," the young man answered.

"So what?" his friend asked gently.

"Space is never empty," the young man answered confidently.

"What does that mean?" his host asked in a non-confrontational tone.

"Let me illustrate my answer. As you know, the first stop was a warehouse," the visitor began. "I went to the side door and walked into a large 'empty' space. It was a very big room. I looked around for a long time before I realized the answer to your question, 'What's in the room?' I was in the room, only me, all alone. The importance of that idea didn't occur to me until later. But I was sure of the answer.

"When I went to the park on a Saturday morning, it was filled with people, literally hundreds of mostly energetic people. But that answer was too obvious. Then as I sat there, I realized that the 'space' was filled with others, who were not me. At the time, even though you had suggested otherwise, I couldn't see any relationship to the mirror. But I still felt good about my answer. Wanting to capture what was happening in the park, I immediately made notes in my journal about the various groups of people. There was simply too much happening to trust my memory.

"Finally, I went to the garden property. I sat in the meadow for a long time. I could hear birds singing. The spring flowers were in bloom and their beauty was breathtaking. The fragrance was sweet enough to lift my spirits, but distant enough not to overpower the moment. After sitting for a while, I opened the envelope and reread the question: What do you feel? I felt peaceful, serene, calm. I stayed there a long time and let the feelings soothe my soul. Because of those feelings, I knew what was there. I didn't need to be asked. God was in that space. He was there in all of His remarkable creations, and He was there in the peace that came into my heart.

"That evening as I sat at my kitchen table with the box, the mirror, the hourglass and my journal in front of me, I asked myself: What do I know about each of these gifts? And how are they related to each other and to my questions?"

"And what were your answers?" his friend asked.

"I am learning that the three significant dimensions of life are time, self, and space, not empty space but space filled with me, others, and God and His creations. While reading my notes from the park, I thought about the words on the mirror, 'What you see is not all of me.' You said I might understand the mirror better when I was in the park. So, I looked for some connecting pattern among the groups of people. I remembered a father lifting a teary-eyed child and comforting him. I thought of the woman sitting in the center of the park, alone, reading a book. And the memory of several schoolchildren playing a pickup soccer game came to mind. Then it hit me. There are three parts to each of us: the heart—a father comforting a child; the mind—a woman reading a book; and the body—children playing a game.

"I couldn't see the three parts just by looking in the mirror. Nevertheless, I realized that I must give consideration to all three parts of myself and others in all of my endeavors and associations. Even if I can't see them, they are always there. And finally, I am learning that when I seek truth, I'll recognize it when I feel peaceful, calm, and reassured. If I ignore those feelings, I'll lose my way. It's somewhat like a compass, I think."

"My, you've come a long way in a short time," his friend exuded reassuringly. "In these weeks, you've also begun to regain your self-confidence. That alone is a powerful achievement. But what about the answers to your questions? You do remember them don't you?"

"How can I not remember them?" he asked honestly. "Some days I think of little else. They run through my mind as if on a wheel. Will God forgive me? Can I recover? Can I ever repair the damage I've caused or do anything of value in others' lives?"

"And what are your answers?" his friend asked.

"I believe the solutions can be found in the gifts you gave me, though I have hardly begun to find them. I'm sure that it will take time, a lot of it, to find affirmative answers to these questions. It will also take all of me—heart, mind, and body. And I will have to give all of myself away to that which fills the space of life—me, others, and God and His creations. Fortunately for those who are listening, the space of life is filled with subtle sounds of guidance, inspiration to lead them to the truth."

After listening carefully, the host said, "I'm delighted with what's happening to you. You have begun to gain a renewed understanding of the three 'dimensions of life.' Now it's time to deepen that understanding. As you've learned, I rarely give answers, only the means to find them. I've leaned that discovery is a good teacher, usually much better than a lecture. That way you find your own answers, not someone else's. And when you make those

13

discoveries, you own them. As you continue your journey, I want to give you a final gift. This is the most important one. Its meaning should be obvious, given your experience in the meadow. And without this gift, all the others are meaningless theories about our condition here on the earth."

After handing the young man a small wrapped box, the host encouraged him to open it. Anxiously, the guest unwrapped the gift and carefully opened the cardboard container. Inside was a mariner's compass with a gold-plated needle pointing confidently in one direction. The handcrafted compass was old and worn. It had probably guided a real searcher on a long and treacherous journey. An inscription of the back of the compass read: *The direction is true when the compass guides the traveler.*

After allowing the young man sufficient time to study the compass, the host made his final request of the evening. "May I suggest you go to the meadow in time to see the sunrise. I have been there as dawn awakens the day. It is always a profound experience. Often our clearest insights come as the day breaks. If you could go tomorrow morning, I think you would find your time well spent. We can meet after you've been to the meadow again."

2

Return to the Meadow

The young man arrived at the meadow the very next day, just before sunrise. Spreading his blanket on the grass, he opened his briefcase, took out the hourglass, and stood it on the blanket just as the first rays of sunlight illuminated the darkened sky. The natural beauty of the setting and his peaceful feelings were enhanced by the silent invasion of light. For a moment it seemed as if the trees were struggling to hold back the dawn as brilliant pink and red streaks raced across the darkened sky, but on it came, relentlessly. The sunlight darted through the leaves and limbs pushed shadows every which way, then illumination overpowered the resistance and the whole meadow filled with light. As a calm feeling of warmth engulfed him, the image of the compass crossed his mind.

Lying on the blanket, he began to study the movement of sand through the hourglass as the sun rose slowly over the tops of the trees. He watched intently as the particles and their shadows struggled through the small opening then dropped silently into the space below. He pondered the meaning of the "present moment" and its importance in his quest for change. He was comforted because, for the first time in a very long while, he really did feel at peace as he thought about his future.

He opened his journal and was just beginning to write when he heard a car door close. After some time, he could hear someone walking slowly along the path. He looked up and saw a woman entering the meadow. She was on crutches and he immediately noticed the sole of her left shoe. It was about four inches thick. The other shoe had a normal sole. The woman struggled as she spread out the blanket she had carried in a pouch tied to one of the crutches. She also removed a journal from the pouch.

He tried not to stare and was a little embarrassed when he realized he should have offered to help. It was obvious that she was trying not to interrupt his writing. But when she saw he was looking toward her, she smiled and asked, "I hope it's okay that I'm here this morning. I don't want to bother you."

"Oh, it's no bother. I'm just a guest here myself," he answered. He thought she wanted to be alone too, so he returned quickly to his journal. His eyes, however, had their own agenda as he kept sneaking peeks at her while he wrote. He soon noticed that her fingers on both hands were gnarled, making writing difficult.

Now, completely distracted, he laid his journal on his lap and asked, "I'm sorry to interrupt, but I think we both surprised each other this morning."

Her smile seemed genuine as she answered. "I think you're right. Have you been coming here long?"

"No, not really," he answered. "This is only my second trip. And you?"

"I've been coming here a long time. I usually come every Saturday, just after dawn." As she was speaking she noticed the hourglass and said, "I think we have a common friend. Where did you buy your hourglass? It looks like a perfect replica of the original."

Puzzled by the question, the young man answered cautiously, "Our friend helped me. I'm not sure where it came from. You'll have to ask him."

Accepting his answer, the woman changed the subject. "If I may ask, what are you learning from your bottle of time? An hourglass is such a rich metaphor. I suppose one could talk about it for hours upon hours."

Though he was normally a private person, he was intrigued by her question about his "bottle of time." He decided to let her come into his world, just a little. "Mostly I've been thinking about the three dimensions of time. You know, past, present and future."

"Have you come to any conclusions?"

"No conclusions really, but I love to watch the future race toward the present, pause, and then suddenly become the past. Sometimes I've laid on my bed as I'm falling asleep and tried to see the place where the past, present, and future touch each other. I haven't caught them yet," he said with a slight smile, "but I haven't given up."

"Do you have any other thoughts about time?" she asked gently.

Once the conversation began, the young man was so immersed in it that he completely forgot the woman's physical difficulties. Instead he continued, "Since I was given the hourglass, I find myself thinking about time quite a lot. For example, if I think about the present, right here in the meadow, I see you. And I wonder how our paths crossed."

"You have an interesting way of expressing yourself," she responded. "And I have to admit, I wonder about our being here at the same time, too. Perhaps it's an omen of good luck for both of us. I feel comfortable talking to you, so I'll tell you a little more about how I came to the meadow the first time. I think that's why I'm here today.

"A long time ago, our friend introduced me to this place. I was young at the time, about fourteen. Until I was twelve, I was as healthy as anyone my age. About that time, I started having severe pain in the joints all over my body. I was diagnosed with an extreme case of juvenile arthritis. It acted quickly. It was also painful and very debilitating. The joints in my knees and hips were soon affected and in less than two years, I was unable to run or play with everyone else. I began to limp and walk slowly. Some people avoided me; I was too much of a bother.

"As you might expect, I gradually became bitter and angry. By the time I was sixteen, my parents found me unbearable. Knowing the reputation of our guide, they asked him to speak with me. He was slow to criticize; instead he used his 'treasures' to help me see what the future held if I continued to be sour and difficult. He also helped me discover that I have the power to change my attitude. It took a lot of trips to the meadow before the peace that's here found a place in my heart. Along the way I've learned that happiness is a choice, not just an automatic response to pleasant circumstances. I found that it shouldn't matter what happens to me; what matters is how I choose to react. Now, I choose to be happy. Sometimes when I'm having an especially bad time physically, I forget my commitment. Then I call our host, and he suggests I revisit the meadow. That's why I'm here today."

The young man was stunned by the woman's honesty as well as her story. "I think you're right; it is a blessing that we both came today. At least that's true for me."

"Well, enough about why I'm here," the woman responded boldly. "Let's go back to the hourglass. What else have you learned about time?"

As he looked at the hourglass, the young man realized the peaceful feeling that accompanied his first visit to the meadow was there in abundance again. He was glad he had come.

"As I said earlier, I see the hourglass displaying past, present, and future in very close proximity. However, I've usually kept it simple and thought about each dimension separately. Because of my particular circumstances, I've thought a lot about the past. Sometimes it's a hard place to visit." He realized it felt good to talk with someone else,

18

someone who understood what he was thinking about because in her own way, she had been there too.

"I've learned you have to be selective when you visit the past," she said contemplatively. "Some of the 'old grains' are more useful than others. Some of them simply have to be left alone. It took me a while to learn which experiences from my past have the most value. Over the years, I've found it useful to record the most important memories—'moments of learning' some have called them. However, finding these significant moments in your past is much different than making a simple journal entry. Most journal writing is recording recent thoughts, feelings, and events."

"I'm not sure what you mean," the young man said.

"Unlike normal journal writing, you have to search your past for the real moments of learning. Once you find them, you have to review the experience to find what was there for you to learn. I imagine you have many such moments of learning in your past that may help you understand the purpose of your life more completely. For me, I think it's best to examine happy memories first. I've also found I can examine an event more clearly if I write about it as an observer rather than as a participant. Something about a different perspective, I think. Not everyone enjoys that approach, but I've always wanted to be a creative writer. Writing in this way helps satisfy the urge."

The young man was deeply impressed by the demeanor of the woman in the midst of such apparent difficulties. No sense of discouragement, only hope and joy came from her tone of voice. He made special note that his feelings of discouragement had diminished while they were talking.

Suddenly, the woman's countenance changed to a look of concern. "Oh my goodness, look at the sun. It's climbed a long way up that eastern sky, and I have an appointment at ten-thirty." Checking her watch, she added, "Oh dear, I'm going to be late. But it's been worth it. I don't tell that story often, but today was easy." She immediately started gathering her things, but this time he was on his feet, helping. He noticed every step, watching her careful placement of the tip of each crutch along the way.

As they were leaving the meadow, she looked back at his hourglass. "I can't believe how much yours looks like the original. But I know he'd never let his heirlooms out of his study."

He didn't know how to respond to her comment, so he said something about the beautiful morning instead.

When she was safely in her car, the young man returned to the meadow. Deciding to stay a while longer and write in his journal, he opened to the first empty page. However, there were too many subjects running through his mind to write a coherent sentence: the beauty of the sunrise; the consistent feeling of peace in the meadow; happiness is a choice, not a reflex; moments of learning can be used to guide the present and the future....

Unable to stop his mind from racing from subject to subject, he gathered up his blanket and headed to the car. He thought he might be reaching a turning point in his journey. Perhaps he was right.

3

The Dinner Party

No sooner had he arrived at his apartment than the phone rang. It was his mentor. "I had a call this morning from a good friend of mine. She told me she met you in the meadow this morning. I was hoping that would happen sometime."

"I really enjoyed talking with her," the young man answered. "Her thoughts were impressive, and her attitude was truly inspiring. She gives the credit to you and her parents."

"That's just like her," the friend responded honestly, "always deferring to others. Execution is the most important thing, however. Without execution, ideas just lie dormant, having little or no value."

"What do you mean?" the young man asked, wanting to hear more of the woman's story.

"Okay, I'll give you a simple example, the more profound ones would take too long to explain." the mentor responded. "Did she talk with you about moments of learning? It's one of her favorite subjects"

"Why yes, she did."

"Well, that's an idea I learned years ago. Simply put, the idea is that you review your past and find meaning in the events. Then, if you're inclined, write them down and analyze what's there to learn. If you don't want to write the event in detail, write your analysis anyway. But she really advanced the concept."

"How so?" he asked, listening intently.

"First, she suggested we should thoroughly search our past. She thinks that the ebb and flow of each person's life is not accidental. Rather, a kind creator put us here to learn important lessons. He set up the apparently random circumstances of life to instruct us; so we shouldn't be surprised to find that life's path is full of these moments of learning. I'm inclined to agree with her. The sad part is, if we aren't paying attention, we'll miss the lesson. It's not too difficult to pick out the big ones, but the little ones have meaning, too. Are you thinking about searching for the moments of learning in your life?"

"Yes. In fact I've already started. I love to write, so I'm using the objective approach she suggested. I'll look at some of my moments of learning as if I were a fly on the wall watching the event."

"Sounds like a good idea. I'd like to read it when you finish, if it's not too personal," his friend replied thoughtfully.

"I'd like that," the young man answered. "I'm going to follow her advice and find a happy moment for the first one. I should finish it in the next few days, and I'll bring it along to our next meeting."

"That brings up my next subject," the older man suggested. "I'd like you to meet some other friends of mine. I'm having a dinner party next Tuesday. Can you join us?"

"Sure, I'd love to come," the student replied.

"Great. Dinner will be served at seven-thirty."

"Okay. Sounds like the party will be fun," the young man answered quickly.

When he hung up the phone, he noticed the light flashing on his answering machine. Pushing the play button, he heard a familiar voice, "Hi, Buv." He smiled at the reminder of his younger brother's pet name for him, a childhood butchering of the word brother. "It's me, Rian. I'm looking forward to your coming down here and setting up your business in my area. I was hoping it would be sooner than later. This young college stud could use the cash. I know you're busy, but I'll make you rich, I promise! Call me."

Deciding to return the call the next day, he turned to the pile of work he'd brought home—then promptly forgot the call.

The days passed quickly and the young man soon found himself pulling up to his friend's house. He was surprised to see so many cars in the circular driveway. For some reason it made him nervous. He wondered if it was because he was used to being alone with his mentor, engaged in private conversations. Soon he was in a crowded family room where the sounds of laughter and enjoyment would make even the most stoic visitor relax. There were conversations of every kind: sports, local politics, family updates, and neighborhood concerns, to mention just a few. The young man met many of the guests. He saw the woman from the meadow across the room. She waved, but before he could make his way to her, the host asked everyone to take their places for dinner.

In no time, all were seated in the spacious dining room. Two large banquet-style tables in the middle of the room accommodated the entire group. The lively conversation didn't subside, but continued right through the meal. The young man was pleased to discover that the woman from the meadow was sitting across the table and one person down from him. After saying hello to her, he met a couple from a nearby city who were also seated across the table.

Before he had finished introducing himself to everyone at the table, the man seated beside him looked across the table at the couple and asked, "Say, Ron, do you still sing in the shower?"

His wife interrupted, "Ron, can I tell them?"

Ron shook his head pleasantly and said, "Why not? You tell everybody else."

His wife then explained, "Ron sings every morning in the shower, every single morning. And he has a terrible singing voice. It's really bad."

"Well, what does he sing?" asked a guest.

"We really don't know. You can't tell, because nobody in the family recognizes the tune. But," she said, "I'm going to tell you something about my husband. Every morning when he comes out of the shower, he is a different man than when he went in."

"Yeah, he's clean," offered the guest.

"Not exactly," his wife responded quickly. "Have you ever seen that soap commercial where the guy who can barely drag himself out of bed goes into the shower? He turns on both faucets, and when the water comes on, he grabs this new soap. He takes a whiff of the soap and then lathers himself all over. By the end of the shower, he's a different person. He's on fire! Well, that's what Ron looks like when he comes out of the shower every morning. He's enthusiastic, he's inspired, and he's ready to meet the day.

"Some of our kids have started singing in the shower like their dad. Thankfully, they didn't inherit his singing voice!"

When his wife had finished, the guest suggested, "Why don't you explain to our new friend here how you got started singing in the shower."

Ron smiled and explained, "Several years ago, I spent a great deal of time with our host. In the course of our discussions I concluded that even though I placed value on happiness, I wasn't a happy person. Further, with his help, I realized that happiness is a decision, not a condition. In simple terms, I said to myself, 'I've been sad and I've been happy in life. And as I compare the two, happy is better.'

"Then one day I came upon a quotation in a magazine that said, 'We don't sing in the shower because we are happy. We're happy because we sing in the shower.' That started me singing in the shower.

"Now I'm not saying everyone should sing in the shower, but I am saying I took a personal inventory and discovered the reason I wasn't very happy in life was because I thought happiness came from outside of me. I was too concerned about things I really couldn't control, like the behavior of my children, what people said to me at work, the traffic going to and from home, what my boss thought of me. When something went wrong in one of those areas, I became unhappy. Then I realized that happiness comes from within, and I control it. Once I realized happiness is a choice, not a reaction, I opened the door to happiness. Does that make sense?" he asked, looking at the young man.

"I think so. Is there more?"

"Not much. After I made the decision to be happy, I kept looking for ways to keep it going. Singing in the shower is a good way for me. You wouldn't know this, but a lot of the people here have made the same discovery in their own way."

Just at that time someone walked up to Ron and touched him on the shoulder, and the conversation ended. The young man smiled across the table at the woman from the meadow and began thinking of all he had learned from her. His thoughts were soon interrupted by the couple sitting to his left. They had heard him say that he worked with a lot of car dealerships, and they wondered about prices. That wasn't his specialty, but it started another interesting conversation. At the end of the evening, he felt full of energy, even though it was late.

Before he went to bed, he wrote several paragraphs in his journal.

Someone said, "Laughter is the best medicine." Tonight proved that to me. At the dinner party, I met many interesting people. The atmosphere was almost festive.

And it was fun. Imagine grumpy me having fun! Sitting across from a genuinely happy couple only added to my sense of relief. The husband's willingness to playfully describe a serious topic created a powerful moment of learning for me. When I combined the principles he presented with the ideas of the woman in the meadow, I can say I am approaching a breakthrough. For the last year or so, I have been struggling with the sorrow known to those who make big mistakes in their lives. During that time, my life has been painted only gray with no cheerful colors. After today, I choose the colors of my life. To be more specific, here is a list of principles I have seen in action in the lives of very good people, including the couple at the dinner party and the woman from the meadow.

1. *Happiness is a choice, not a response to my situation.*
2. *No matter how difficult my circumstances, others have struggled with worse and found the way to be happy.*
3. *Even though I am wrestling with a lot issues right now, I have the right, perhaps even the obligation, to be happy, to find joy in my life.*
4. *Pain in life is inevitable, but suffering is optional. How I respond is up to me.*

One other thing Ron said that really stands out, "Life is about learning and learning can be fun, if we choose to make it so." I know it won't be easy. I know that the woman from the meadow has bad days too. I'll do my best to find happiness and joy in my journey.

Now a word or two about the gifts. Each has a symbolic meaning that is helping me understand my life better. To review: The hourglass stands for time—past, present, and future; the mirror is a symbol for all of me—heart, mind, and body. The box is a little more difficult to understand. It represents space, the space that God has filled with me, others, and His marvelous creations. And finally, the compass reminds me that I can be guided on my odyssey by the calm, peaceful feeling I found in the meadow. Along the way, as I discover helpful ideas or principles, I will use these four treasures as a guide to understanding. Starting tonight, I'll highlight entries about the gifts so I can find them later. I already have two thoughts that are symbolic of the hourglass and the mirror.

<u>The Hourglass</u>: Moments of learning are usually found in the past but sometimes they are recognized as they happen, in the present. For example, I experienced a moment of learning in the present as Ron told his story about singing in the shower. I didn't have to search the past for it. This moment of learning was set in place by my mentor. However, I had to be willing to let it happen and learn from it or it would be of no value. Also, by the time I wrote about this moment of learning in my journal, it was an event from my past, even though it was recorded on the same day. The passing of time between the dinner party and this time of writing has allowed me the opportunity to consider the meaning of the event more thoroughly.

<u>The Mirror</u>: I've learned that choices are made inside of me. What I mean is that I am most successful with my choices when I engage all of me—heart, mind, and body—in the effort. So, the symbolism of the mirror—what you see is not all of me—is helpful when considering the lessons learned at the dinner party tonight. For example, I was reminded that happiness is a choice. If I am to truly find happiness, I must enlist all of myself—my heart, mind, and body—in the quest.

Finishing his writing, the young man closed his journal and placed a manila envelope on top of it. His mentor had given it to him as he left the house. There was a note paper-clipped to the envelope that read: "My young friend: I thought about asking you to stay a while after everyone left so we could talk, but my wife reminded me it would be late and I need my rest. Sometimes she acts like I'm eighty-five and in failing health when in truth, I just turned fifty-nine in December! However, I took her counsel seriously and wrote you a note instead. In this envelope is a story I wrote a long time ago. It's a true story. I hope you find it helpful. It looked like you were enjoying the conversations with your dinner companions. I'd love to hear of your experiences sometime soon. Please call me when it's convenient. I enjoy our visits." It was signed, "Your friend and fellow traveler."

Eager to read the story, but knowing it would be better after a good night's rest, he put the envelope on the nightstand and went to bed, but not without looking at the envelope again and wondering . . . .

4

Discovering the Truth

The next morning the young man awoke early. Settling himself in a comfortable chair, he took his friend's story out of the envelope and began to read.

It's Not About Girls

"Hey Mom, I got chosen for the city competition," an enthusiastic voice exclaimed as the eleven-year-old boy crashed through the door and spilled into the house.

"That's great, Bobby," his mom responded while trying to slow her child down. "When will it be held?"

"Next Saturday," he said proudly. "And I think I'll win."

"But Bobby," she reacted, "isn't that the day you promised to trim Mrs. Ellington's shrubs."

"Oh, yeah, I forgot. I'll guess she'll have to do it herself," he responded, pleased that he had found a solution so quickly. "Besides, I don't need the money. I can get what I need from you. Just like always."

Not happy with her son's response, but knowing it was a teaching moment, Mary Edwards proceeded slowly, keeping in mind some of the things she knew about her son. "Bobby is quick to action," she thought, "a little slow in thinking things through, but filled with a great big heart." With that thought, she asked, "Bobby, how old is Mrs. Ellington?"

"Oh, I don't know, older than dirt," Bobby answered, disappointed that they were still talking about Mrs. Ellington. "She must be a hundred and twenty, if she's a day," he said, hoping the subject would quickly change to the city competition.

Trying to help things along, he asked, "So what time will we leave Saturday?"

Seeing she was getting nowhere, his mother decided to try a different tack. "What time is the competition on Saturday, Son?"

"About eleven for the kids my age," he answered, pleased that Mrs. Ellington's shrubs had been forgotten.

"And what will you do in the morning before we leave?"

"Study, study, study if I'm going to beat those dumb girls," he answered.

"Good answer," his mom said quickly. "I have an idea. Why don't you go over to Mrs. Ellington's now and tell her you have to be done by ten. Then ask her if she would mind sitting outside while you trim the shrubs and ask you questions to help you prepare for the competition. She's a retired schoolteacher, you know, so I'm sure she'll be a great coach."

Unable to talk his Mom out of the idea, Bobby walked reluctantly over to Mrs. Ellington's house and made the deal. On Saturday morning, after two hours of clipping shrubbery, he knew all the information cold. "And besides," he often explained later, "she paid me for helping me win. What a deal!"

In the city where Bobby grew up, it had become a yearly tradition for sixth graders from all the elementary schools to meet on a Saturday in the spring to demonstrate their proficiency in basic skills. It was a limited program and only a few were chosen from each school. The format was simple. The participant was asked to recite facts about history and geography, repeat math tables, and quote poetry. The goal was to say everything perfectly. Those who were able to do so received a certificate with a gold seal attached and "100%" printed on it. There were also "90%" and "75%" seals. As he left home at ten-thirty that Saturday, Bobby was sure he would get the one hundred percent certificate.

At exactly eleven o'clock, a teacher stood up in front of the school auditorium and announced the classroom assignments. Bobby noticed two girls from his school looking furtively at him. He thought he heard one of them say, "If he gets a seventy-five percent sticker, I'll be surprised."

Bobby flushed; he wondered why girls always treated him that way. "They think they're so smart. Well, I'll show them," he said to no one in particular as he gritted his teeth and followed his group down a long hallway into a classroom.

What Bobby didn't hear was the girl's real comment. "If he gets a seventy-five percent sticker, I'll be surprised. He must be the smartest boy in any sixth grade in the city."

"Yeah," said the other girl. "But he never pays attention to us."

With that, the two girls joined their group and walked down the same hallway to a classroom directly across from the one Bobby had just entered. Both girls were excellent students and volunteered to be first, hoping to be in the hall when Bobby got out.

In the meantime, a perspiring Bobby Edwards watched two students from another school recite the required material as if they had written it themselves. "Who's next?" asked the teacher, an old woman Bobby thought looked like the Wicked Witch of the East. "Right out of *The Wizard of Oz*," he thought silently. "That stare could freeze a bonfire."

"How about you, young man," she asked in a voice that made his blood run cold.

"Who me?" he responded. Then, remembering Mrs. Ellington's parting words, "You're ready to conquer the world, Bobby. I'm sure you'll be a champion," his confidence suddenly returned, and Bobby strode quickly to the front of the room.

"Start with the poetry, Bobby," the wicked witch suggested, mocking him for sure, he thought.

"Let nothing upset you, Son," Mrs. Ellington had said. "When you're prepared, you don't have to fear."

"I have chosen *Paul Revere's Ride* by Henry Wadsworth Longfellow, "Listen, my children, and you shall hear, Of the midnight ride of Paul Revere," Bobby began without a trace of fear in his voice.

Seven minutes and several topics later, the teacher, with eyes that suggested she was going to put him in boiling water for spite said, "You recited everything perfectly, young man. Congratulations. You'll receive a one hundred percent sticker in the awards ceremony right after lunch. We'll see you then."

Bobby burst out the door with both hands in the air. "Yes!" He exclaimed, "I did it."

Looking up, he saw those same two girls who had made fun of him earlier. "I'm going to get even right now," he promised himself as he walked up to them, "and I know just the way," he added, grabbing two purses sitting on a window ledge.

They pretended not to notice as he approached. Suddenly, Bobby turned and started to walk away quickly. The girls, troubled by his departure, decided to follow after him. Down the hall he went, looking over his shoulder.

"Darn," he exclaimed, "they're coming after me and they're catching up. I didn't expect that. Maybe their purses are slowing me down."

He picked up speed. So did they. Coming to a set of stairs, he decided to go to the top and find a place to hide. Looking back, he saw they were still gaining on him. "Boy, these purses are heavier than I thought. I'm gonna have to get rid of them real soon. If I make them spend a little time looking, maybe they'll leave me alone from now on."

Looking up the stairs again, he was sure they wouldn't follow him into unknown territory. And he was pleased that the stairs weren't carpeted because he was certain that tiled stairs with metal strips at the front edge were a lot easier to climb.

As he began his ascent, Bobby had a vague memory of having been on the second floor before. But this time the lights were off and there were no windows anywhere. The hallway was pitch black. "This is great," he thought. "All girls are afraid of the dark. I've heard that somewhere. So now I've lost them for sure. But just in case, I better get into that other hallway. It's about halfway down, I think. I'll dart in there and slip into a classroom. They'll never find me."

Quickly, he raced down the dark hallway and made an abrupt left. No sooner had he turned the corner and taken two giant steps than he realized he had just entered a stairwell, not a hallway. To make it worse, it was an uncarpeted, tiled stairwell with rough metal strips across the

32

front of each step. Gravity immediately took over and down Bobby plummeted, head over heels over purses. Unfortunately, at the bottom of the stairs was a solid oak door, securely closed. Bobby hit the door with a resounding thud. As he tried to stand up, the door opened and a bright flood of light illuminated the stairwell. Standing in the doorway was the Wizard of Oz himself, disguised as the building custodian.

"What's going on here," he bellowed in a very gruff voice.

Still trying to sort it out himself, Bobby stammered, "I'm not exactly sure." At the same time, he was casually using his feet to push the purses out of sight.

"Well you're the only one here, so you must know what happened."

"I guess I fell down the stairs," Bobby answered, still a little worried about the purses.

"Don't ever do that again," the wizard commanded, turning as if to close the door.

"But I thought it was a hallway," Bobby responded defensively.

"Well, it isn't a hallway. It's never been a hallway; it's always been a stairwell. As long as I've been here, it's been a stairwell."

Bobby couldn't even imagine how long that was. The ancient one just kept talking.

"Your problem, young man, is you didn't believe it was a stairwell. And now you just learned something that a lot of kids never catch on to. Some things are true whether you believe them or not. The sooner you get that into your head, the better off you'll be." With that, the custodian slammed the door and locked it again, without even asking Bobby if he was hurt.

But the stairwell was no longer dark. Dark halls are no obstacles for girls when light switches are nearby. Looking up, Bobby saw the two girls. "Are you alright?" asked one.

By this time, Bobby had dusted himself off and was marching back up the stairs, purses in hand, holding them out in front of him with a sheepish look on his face.

"That was a fun race," said the other girl, "and you beat us. So how did you do in the competition, Bobby?"

Handing the girls their purses when he got to the top, Bobby answered, "I earned a one hundred percent sticker."

"We knew you'd do it," said one.

"Why you're one of the smartest boys in the whole school," the said other.

Bobby felt his face flush and wondered what was happening. He seemed to have made a mistake about both the 'hallway' *and* the girls. That stairwell had always been a stairwell; and these girls had always liked him. As *The Wizard of Oz* custodian had just taught him: *Some things are true whether you believe them or not."*

Placing the story on the table, the young man wondered what the writer's conclusion had to do with his journey and the answers to his questions. Throughout the day, he thought about the statement: "Some things are true whether you believe them our not." He tried to find exceptions to the underlying idea. He asked himself if belief ever determined actual truth. Not able to come up with any examples, he decided he'd call his friend when he got home and talk with him about the story.

At the end of the day, excited to make the phone call, he drove straight home. As he plunged through the front door, he noticed the message light was blinking on his phone. Curious, because he wasn't expecting any calls, he pressed the "play" button.

"Hey, Buv, it's me, Rian, your long-lost and struggling little brother. I'm down here at school watching my funds dwindle, wondering when you're going to break away and come teach me the business. Remember, I can make you rich. Really, I don't mean to be a bother. I know you've got a lot on your mind, but when you get time, I'm ready to rumble, as in learn to sell your great product. Love ya."

Embarrassed he still hadn't called his brother, he promised himself he would fix it right after he ate. During the meal, he thought about the stairwell story and smiled when he imagined the shock of falling down a "hallway." He became intrigued with the possible application to his life. Picking up the phone, he called his friend. "I read your story today," he began, "and I have lots of questions. The first one is about what you learned by writing this as an observer."

"Fair enough," the older man answered. "That's a good place to start. I learned a lot about Mrs. Ellington. I learned for example, that she was a very good person, one willing to help when I needed help. And I've realized that I probably didn't do much of a job on her shrubs, but she didn't care as much about them as she did about me. I learned that my mother wanted me to get acquainted with a remarkably thoughtful person. When I thought about it later, I could remember that Mrs. Ellington often came out to talk with me about my schoolwork when I worked on her shrubs. Over the years, it has occurred to me that the 'space of my life' is filled with wonderful people, I just have to look for them.

"I also learned that the so-called competition wasn't competition at all. It was a means used by the school district to get us to memorize concepts and facts that would stay with us the rest of our lives. Even today, I can still recite *Paul Revere's Ride*.

"And I learned that there was a commendable quality of service in the efforts of schoolteachers who donated a Saturday for our sake. I learned that the custodian was indeed a lot like the Wizard of Oz. He was all bluff and bluster that day, but when I made it to junior high, he became a good friend. In fact, he was one of the nicest adults at the school, always helping students, especially the needy ones. There's a lot of wisdom in a custodian who spends his lifetime in dungarees keeping the hallways clear and helping students find their way.

"One other thing, I learned that when I write as an observer, I can use the story without drawing attention to myself. That has often been quite useful. The list of what I learned by being the observer is much longer, but that's a start."

"That's a good list," the young man said. "I'll have to think about it. Now I have a few other questions. They all center on the custodian's statement, "Some things are true whether you believe them or not." I wonder about that statement. But mostly I wonder why you gave me this particular story. From your perspective, how does the story apply to my circumstances?"

Appreciating the question, the older man continued, "My answer starts with the idea that our lives are governed by immutable principles. They are immutable because they are true, and they never change. If we lose track of these principles, the time will come when we will suddenly fall into a dark stairwell, and all the believing and hoping for a hallway will be to no avail. There will be nothing there to save us. But there will always be people standing at the bottom, pointing out the obvious."

"That's easy to say, but hard to achieve," the young man observed. "How can anyone know with certitude if they've found the truth?"

"Well, we're talking because there was a time when you ignored the truth about things you already knew. And now you know with certitude that you've fallen down a stairwell that you pretended or hoped was a hallway. Isn't that so? Your questions center on how to get back up the stairs in such a way that will allow you to recover some, if not all, of what you lost."

Although he was a little uncomfortable with his friend's directness, the young man agreed that there was truth in what he said. "So where do I go from here?" he asked, wondering if he was being told that his desires were impossible.

"That's always the question," the gray-haired man answered. "Where do I go from here? I guess my suggestion is a simple one. You continue on the path you're on. Keep in mind your feelings in the meadow as you search for truth, for the answers to your questions. You'll find a way. I am confident of that.

"The next step may be to search your life for a moment of learning and write it down. Perhaps you'd like to experiment by writing it as an observer. What do you think?" the older man concluded.

"I think that's a good idea," the young man answered. "We've covered a lot tonight, but I still have more questions. I want to talk about the dinner party and what happened there. However, I think I'd rather have that conversation in person."

"That works for me," said the mentor. "Why don't you write your story, and when you've finished we can get together."

Each hung up his phone, wondering what the young man would find by searching his past.

Later that evening, he returned to his journal.

*The Box: I am beginning to enjoy looking at important experiences through the lenses provided by the gifts. It adds perspective. And it's fun to decide which gift is the most helpful in understanding a moment of learning. It's challenging to choose the right gift for the story, "It's Not About Girls." The story's conclusion, **Some things are true whether you believe them or not**, is easy to say, but not so easy to see. And when it's applied in my life, it's painful to think about. I got caught in the trap of believing in and acting upon ideas that simply weren't true. I must have thought I was exempt from the consequences. And, as was pointed out by my friend, it really cost me. When we got into the discussion about how I had ignored the truth in* *my life, I was totally affected, heart, mind, and body, but especially in my heart. It was a very painful discussion. So why have I chosen the box as the gift to use with the story instead of the mirror? Because the story is about truth, not my mistakes. Truth transcends time, eliminating the hourglass; and truth cannot be changed by my heart, mind or body, eliminating the mirror. Truth stands independent in the space that God has provided. So, the box is the best choice.*

One other thought—I've heard it said that sometimes the truth hurts. What should be added is that just because the truth hurts doesn't make it false. I am convinced that I will only be able to amend for the mistakes I've made by being aware of the stairwells of life and not pretending they're hallways.

As he closed his journal, the young man considered what he needed to do next. Remembering he'd been encouraged to discover moments of learning in his past, he fell asleep trying to remember some. He was about to make another important turn in his journey.

5

Searching the Past

For the next several evenings, the young man thoughtfully examined his past. He would lie on his bed, close his eyes, and methodically review his life. He tried to remember the time before he was in school. At first not much was pulled from the recesses of his mind, only what he'd been told by others along with vague memories of his earliest days. As he continued to search, however, he was surprised to find events coming more and more into view. Even some of those early times seemed to have meaning and importance. He made a brief note in his journal about each event as he remembered it, so he could recall it later.

He continued grade by grade, summer by summer, thinking, remembering, visualizing, and writing notes. When he got past the sixth grade, he decided to choose one happy event from his first eleven years and write about it. After a few days, he finished the task and chose a title.

The Tetherball Game

The towheaded eight year old sneaked carefully out the back door and was tiptoeing down the steps when his mother's voice rang out. "Tommy, do you have your homework done? If not, please come back and finish it."

"How does she do that when she can't even see me?" Tommy wondered, as he turned around and slowly walked back through the door. Slamming his math book on the table, he pulled a wrinkled piece of notebook paper out of his back pocket, smoothed it out, took a pencil stub from his front pocket, then stared blankly at the assignment he had scribbled down at school. It read: "page 11, problems 1-10, page 12, problems 5-12, and story problems 13-15."

"I hate homework," Tommy mumbled under his breath as he slowly turned to page eleven. "All I ever do is homework, and all I *want* to do is go out and play. Freddie Martino just got a new tetherball pole, and here I am, stuck in the house," he added loudly as his mother walked into the room.

"Tommy, I have an idea," his mother offered.

Wincing in anticipation, Tommy asked cautiously, "Yeah, what kind of idea, Mom?"

"Well, you know I've told you that you can do anything for one minute," his mother began pleasantly and then for emphases added, "No matter how difficult the event, you can endure it for a minute."

"Sure, Mom," he answered glumly. "You've told me that a million times. It comes up whenever I have a dentist appointment, when I have to eat my broccoli, or when I'm supposed to be nice to my sisters. But I just want to go play tetherball, not do something I hate!"

"Here's the idea," his mom continued as she opened the cupboard and took out a timer. "This time, let's think of doing something difficult for *five* minutes and mix it with something fun. You sit here at the counter, do your homework for five minutes, and then you can go out and play for five minutes. What do you think?"

Tommy's eyes lit up at the thought. "That's a great idea, Mom. You're a genius!" The eight year old ripped open his math book and started writing the answer to a problem on his wrinkled paper while his mother set the timer for exactly five minutes.

The time raced by as the young student worked feverishly. He knew he had to make an honest effort, or Mom would call the whole thing off. When the timer rang, Tommy had only completed three problems, but that seemed like a lot to him. Immediately, he jumped up from the chair, bolted out the door, and raced across the street to Freddie Martino's home. It was two houses up from his place, but he covered the distance in record time. Tommy was still pounding on the front door when Freddie opened it. "What's up?" he asked, puzzled by his friend who was leaning against the bricks, huffing and puffing.

"We don't have time to talk," Tommy responded, grabbing Freddie's arm and pulling him out the door. "We've got to get to the tetherball stand. And we have no time to lose!"

Eight year olds are used to odd behavior. They've all engaged in it enough to think it's pretty normal. So Freddie followed Tommy into the side yard and they immediately began to play. It seemed to both of them that they had no sooner started when a bold, piercing voice shattered the game. "T - ah - mie."

Without a word, Tommy stopped playing and headed for home. He knew if he didn't follow the plan, his mother would veto it, and he'd be back in the kitchen staring at his math book with no hope of playing. As he left Freddie's yard, he shouted instructions over his shoulder, "Freddie, don't leave! I'll be right back."

Freddie stood there a little confused, but not dumbfounded. After all, they were both eight and still trying to figure things out.

In no time Tommy was sitting at the table hurriedly writing the answers to problems four through seven. Just as he wrote the answer to number seven, the timer rang and Tommy leaped from his chair. "I'm outa here," he exclaimed, hitting the door with maximum force. His mom only smiled as she reset the timer. One thought passed quickly through Tommy's mind as he zoomed out: Was it a little unfair that the timer was reset for playing time just as he left the house, while on the other hand, math time didn't begin until he had his book open? At that moment, though, there was no time to renegotiate the rules; there was tetherball to play.

Tommy must have broken his own best record in the race to Freddie's house, because they were back into the tetherball game before the timer hit thirty seconds. This time Freddie had a real advantage, as Tommy's heavy breathing was the outward sign of a tiring opponent. The first round had ended in a tie, zero to zero. But this second round the score was two to zero in Freddie's favor when the sounds of battle were interrupted by, "T – ah - mie!"

"Don't go away," the fatigued combatant asserted, dashing across the street in full gallop. And he wasn't hurt too much when his brakes failed on the glazed brick porch, and he slid into the door at full speed. Undaunted, he ripped the door open, ran to his chair and opened the book, starting at problem number eight.

"Oh, this is going great," his mom offered, smiling. "And it looks like you're having a real good time at Freddie's." Tommy wasn't sure, but he didn't have time to analyze it right then. There was math to do and more tetherball to play.

After the next round, with Freddie ahead five to zero, Tommy decided to answer through his labored breathing when his mother asked, "So how is this working out for you, son?"

"Not so good," he responded. He looked carefully at the assignment list and offered an alternative. "Mom, why don't I just finish my homework? There are only ten problems left. I can do them in no time and then go finish the game."

"What a great idea, Son. If that's what you want to do, that's fine with me," his mother responded, turning away to hide a smile.

As soon as he finished his homework, Tommy slammed his math book closed with an air of finality and shouted, "Hey Mom, I'm finished!" Jumping from his chair and hitching up his Levis, he dashed confidently to the back door, saying out loud to no one in particular, "Now I'm ready for some tetherball!"

Tommy realized that three great things happened that day. First, he got his homework done faster than ever before. Second, he set a personal best for time running to Freddie's house. And finally, he was the victor in the most stunning comeback in tetherball history. He beat Freddie ten to eight. To this day, Freddie denies Tommy's version, but doesn't offer one of his own.

When the young man finished reading his story, he wanted to record what he learned from writing his "happy moment of learning." He quickly opened his journal and smiled as he noted that he was using a pen instead of the stub of a pencil.

Now, as an adult, when I look back on the day of the tetherball game, there are some other insights that I can see. First, a fundamental understanding of time was implanted in my eight-year-old mind: If you can do a difficult thing for one minute, it's not that much harder to stretch the time out a little longer. That's still a good idea, even after all these years. Another thing: Mom showed me it's far better to be allowed to discover the guiding principles of life than it is to have those values imposed. My mentor is using that same technique now. It must still be a good idea. And finally, I learned that you can beat the snot out of a friend in tetherball when you've completed your homework and he hasn't! (I just had to write that sentence.) The excitement of that victory is still stored somewhere close to the surface. It comes back every time I think of the look on Freddie's face when the game was over. But the point is, late in the game, when he knew his mom was going to call him any minute, he started worrying about getting his homework done. It became a distraction. The principle here is: Focus is a key to achieving success.

The Hourglass: I love remembering the day of the famous tetherball game. (At least it's famous to me.) But I want to view that day from another perspective. The hourglass is the symbol of time—past, present, and future. The most important lessons from the tetherball game are about time—in this case, the present. Mom had taught me the principle that you can do anything for one minute many times over. But it really came home to roost that day. I probably began realizing the power of the present moment way back then.

When I look at the hourglass and see a single grain of sand plunge suddenly from the future into the past, I realize everything happens in that brief instant called the present. That's why it's so important to be focused in the present

and not spend too much time in the past or the future. It's
a very delicate balance.

As he put down his pen, he was excited to share these newfound ideas with his mentor. He quickly called and made arrangements to see his friend soon. Knowing from experience that these meetings were always filled with surprises, he hoped the next one would be the same. He was not disappointed.

6

Baby Food

So much had happened since the two were together last that the young man found himself a little anxious as he drove up the street toward his mentor's home. Soon he was standing at the front door, waiting.

"My," his host began as he opened the door, "the expression on your face is as enthusiastic as your voice was on the phone last week! I guess we have a lot to discuss." Leading him into the study, the older man continued, "I think you have the agenda today. Where do you want to start?"

"When I was at the meadow, the woman said something strange about the hourglass. She said mine was an amazing likeness of the original. I wasn't sure what she meant. Is there something I should know?"

"Well, well. She is a curious one. These treasures, as you've called them, are yours to keep. There is a little more to the story, but I'd rather wait a while before I tell you the rest," his mentor responded. "There will be another, better time, and you just need to be patient for now. In the meantime, please feel free to be open and honest about them being yours. They're a gift from me."

"Fair enough," the guest answered thoughtfully.

"Now tell me what else you want to talk about," the host continued. "I've been curious about how things have been going for you."

"I brought a story I've written. No one has read it yet. I wanted you to be the first." The guest pushed a manila folder across the table and added, "I think I'm a little anxious about what you think, so why don't you read it while I look through my journal. There are some entries I'd like to show you."

Nodding his head in agreement, the host began reading. As the young man glanced through his journal, the mentor made comments while he read.

"My, your mother was a teacher after my own heart. That's the great thing about mothers; they know instinctively the right things to do. Teaching you that you can do anything for one minute, no matter the difficulty, was a stroke of genius on her part!"

He turned a page, continuing to make comments as he read. "Imagine, letting an eight year old discover important principles on his own. She had great confidence in you. She was pretty smart, too. You were a sucker for the tetherball game." The older man laughed as he envisioned the eight year old huffing and puffing. He sighed as he finished the story, "If this is an example of what's stored in your memory bank, you have a treasure trove to search. This first story will be worth reviewing from time to time for its value in your life and in the lives of others."

"I'm glad my writing made sense. Now I want to show you something I invented to help me understand my experiences." With that, he opened his journal to the page where he recorded the tetherball story.

"I think it's a useful tool," his friend observed, "to list the name of a gift beside your comments about a moment of learning. It will help you as you write, and perhaps you'll want to refer to it later. You're certainly on the right track using the hourglass image for the lesson your mother taught. To understand the importance of the present moment is critical for a person starting out on a journey like yours. Have you written any other gift entries?"

"Yes, a few others. Would you like to see them?"

Of course, if they're not too personal," the host replied. "If you'd like, I'll give my opinion about your choice of gifts." The young man showed the other entries to his mentor, who read them carefully, making comments as he turned the pages.

"Your observation that moments of learning happen in the present as well as the past is a good insight. Let me whet your curiosity a little. If you continue on this path, you'll find that you can create moments of learning in your future. Some will come along just when you need them."

The young man made a quick note in his journal then turned to another gift entry, passing it to his host.

"You were fortunate our mutual friend was open with you. She's usually slow to talk about herself. There's so much more to her story. She's had more surgeries than I can count, mostly on her hips and knees. Lately, her ability to walk at all has been at risk. The remarkable thing, of course, is her resilient attitude. Doctors call her recoveries a miracle. I think it's a miracle of determination—her will against overpowering odds. She has clearly proven that happiness is a choice, but what can't be so easily seen is that she also has proven that healing is strongly influenced by one's attitude. I certainly agree with your choice of the mirror as the tool best suited to examine her story. She has put all of herself into the demanding conditions of her life. When most of us compare the difficulties of our lives with her situation, we don't have much to feel bad about."

The young man was touched by the new information about the woman in the meadow. "I've appreciated the opportunity to talk with her. I intend to seek her out again. I do have one more gift entry, if you don't mind." After making a quick note of his friend's comments, he turned to the page where he reviewed the story about falling down the stairs.

The older man quickly read the entry. "I couldn't agree more. Truth does transcend time and is unaffected by our thoughts and emotions. I should add that I disagree with the popular idea that perception is reality. Only reality is reality. Otherwise, reality has no meaning. I believe truth is a knowledge of things as they really are, not as we think they are. It appears that you are also coming to similar conclusions. When we spoke about a definition of truth, I know it was hard for you to hear me say you had made some very bad choices. However, it's crucial that you come to know this with all of you—heart, mind, and body—in order to make the kinds of commitments that will ensure that you never repeat the behavior." Closing the journal, the older man congratulated his guest for the remarkable progress he was making.

"There's another topic I'd like to pursue," the mentor suggested, "one that should be included as you build the foundation for the rest of your journey. It happened when I was a young father. Hopefully, I'm a little smarter now.

"Also, as you might expect, because the story is about me, it's in my journal. I've made a copy for you to read. Take your time. I have a phone call to make, so I'll go in the other room and be back in a few minutes." After handing several typewritten pages to his guest, the host quietly left the room.

The young man began reading.

Baby Food

One evening after work, I strolled happily into the kitchen to find my wife and my daughter Amanda glaring at each other. Amanda was in the high chair and my wife, the adult, was standing directly in front of her. I could just feel the tension the moment I entered the room.

So I said to my sweetheart, "What's the matter, Honey?"

"Amanda won't eat her strained spinach."

You should have seen the look on Amanda's face! She was firm in her resolve and looked as though she had lockjaw. My feeling at that time was that adults can surely control the behavior of their children.

So I said in my most helpful tone, "Honey, I'll bet I could get Amanda to eat her strained spinach."

"Fine, Dear, you feed her," she replied as she began a hasty exit from the kitchen.

To make matters worse, I said, "No. No, Honey, stick around, I'd like you to see how to do this."

Whew! Two big mistakes in less than five minutes. But hey, I'm from Mars and she's from Venus and at that time John Gray's book was not yet on the market. Besides, real men didn't need self-help books.

Even though my daughter was only eight months old and couldn't talk, as soon as I saw her face, I imagined I knew exactly what she was thinking. She was looking at me with a look of love all over her face, which said to me "Oh, Daddy, you're here to rescue me. Mom wants me to eat this yucky stuff. I've never seen her eat it. I've never seen you eat it. And I'm not going to eat it."

That's what the look said; still, I thought I was in control. And why was I feeling so confident? Because I knew that with a small child, or even with a grown-up for that matter, you can squeeze their little cheeks on the side and get an opening big enough for a baby spoon. So I walked over to Amanda and very gently squeezed both of her little cheeks together, and sure enough the opening appeared. But the look of love left.

At that precise moment, the look on her face said to me, "You're in cahoots with Mom, aren't you?"

I looked over at my wife and made sure she was watching. I scooped the strained spinach onto the little baby spoon and slid the spoon into the opening I had created. Then, pushing the spoon up next to her gums, I withdrew the spoon. The strained spinach dropped onto her tongue. In my final act of triumph, I sealed her little lips with my thumb and forefinger.

She's got to swallow it. Right?

Three seconds later I discovered what jet propulsion was all about. The spinach exploded right out of Amanda's mouth and all over the front of me.

By then, my wife was nearly on the floor in hysterics as she gasped, "Show me that again."

Trying to recover, I announced boldly, "Honey, Amanda doesn't like strained spinach. So let's not make a big deal about it." And I walked out of the kitchen.

From this simple event, I learned some important lessons. The first was: I don't have control over someone else's behavior, no matter how much older, bigger, or supposedly wiser I am. I simply don't control someone else's behavior. Another lesson came when I asked the question: What do I really control?

To help me, I looked at the gifts, which represent three dimensions of life. In reflecting upon the symbols, I can say I don't control the hourglass, or any of the contents of the box except me. What I do control is what the mirror represents: my behavior, all of me—my thoughts, my feelings, and my actions—heart, mind, and body.

After I came to this understanding, I wanted to be even more specific, so I took a piece of paper, titled it "What Do I Really Control?" and divided it into two sides. On the left side I wrote, "Things I Don't Control." On the right side I wrote, "Things I Do Control". I gathered information for several months by talking with others and continued to think about it myself. Eventually I had a pretty good list, and I've added to it since. I found that most things go on the side called "Things I Don't Control."

On that side, for example I wrote "time." It took me a while to realize that I don't manage or control time. I can't stop it, nor can I speed it up. Its relentless pace is independent of me. So what is time? I believe that time can best be understood as a series of events. Although I can't control or manage time, I can influence events.

I added other items to the side called "Things I Don't Control." For example, the traffic; I don't control the traffic. I also included weather, death and taxes, natural laws like gravity, the tides, the full moon, and the big one—other people's behavior. I don't control other people's behavior. I never have and never will. That's a hard one to remember, but it's true, whether I believe it or not. This list could be longer, but I've covered some important points. On the other side, "Things I Do Control," I could only think of one item: my behavior. That's right, the only thing I control is *my* behavior. That was a great discovery and one that's guided my life for years. When I finished, my list looked like this:

50

What Do I Really Control?

Things I Don't Control	Things I Do Control
Time — Past, Present, or Future	
	My Behavior!
Traffic	
Weather	
Death and Taxes	
Natural Laws—Gravity, etc	
Other People's Behavior	

* * * * * * * *

This simple chart has had a great influence in my life. Once I completed it, I could see again that I don't control time; I don't control anything except me, my behavior. Some of my greatest challenges or difficulties in life have come when I have forgotten which side of the list I should be working on. Often, when I get frustrated or angry, I'm reacting to those things I don't control. When I remember that I should focus on those things I do control (all of me), I find the greatest peace of mind. To be honest, I should add that this is still an ongoing battle, but I'm making good progress.

He finished reading just as his host re-entered the room. "I would love to have been in the room for the spinach explosion," he laughed.

"Only as an observer, I suspect," his friend said with a sheepish grin. "But it was a great moment of learning. These ideas came together as I thought more about my attempt to control Amanda's behavior. Then I began to watch more carefully to see how other people react to the world around them. Gradually, I began to realize that I could save myself a lot of worry and grief if I focused on the things I control. But I still forget and find myself working on the wrong side of the model, but I do keep making progress."

51

At that moment, the host's wife came into the study. "Honey, Ralph Wilcox is on the phone. He says he really needs to talk with you. It sounds urgent. But please be careful what you commit to do."

Looking at his guest, he said, "I'm sorry, but I've forgotten I asked Ralph to call tonight. This has been a good discussion. Let's continue it soon. Can you find your way out?"

"Of course! I really appreciate the time we've spent together tonight. I'll call again in a day or two and make another appointment."

In his journal that night, he wrote:

This has been a good day. I'm amazed at the practical value of what I am learning, though I need to practice the principles more, and not just be impressed by them. I guess I need to get out of the learning mode and into the experimenting mode, or out of the classroom and into the laboratory. I will do it!

I was also impressed with the way my friend juggled a time conflict tonight, using simple courtesy. As I think about the list of people my friend is helping and the variety of their problems, I am reminded that life is filled with unexpected storms. My life has been very peaceful since I've been meeting with him. I'm sure this can't continue long. Life is too uncertain for that. I just hope I'm ready to endure the storms that will inevitably come my way.

7

The Phone Call

It was a Sunday morning the young man would never forget. The persistent ringing of his phone awakened him from a deep sleep. He immediately recognized the voice of his mentor's wife. She sounded alarmed, but not panic-stricken.

"I have difficult news for you. My husband wanted me to call you this morning and ask you to come to the house today. Before you get here, I need to tell you he has an inoperable brain tumor. It was discovered about six months ago. At his insistence, we haven't told anyone but family members. He was sure he would beat it. It started growing again about a month ago. Then last Friday morning, after another round of tests, the doctor told us his time is very short. The tumor has grown much larger, and it's possible that he will lose consciousness soon. He insisted you come to see him today. The meeting will take about an hour. Can you be here soon?"

A time was arranged, and the phone call ended as abruptly as it started. The young man was unable to concentrate. He quickly showered and took out his journal. He wanted to review everything that had happened since he started meeting with his mentor. For a few minutes, he wouldn't allow his mind to explore the obvious questions and issues about his friend's condition. But eventually they came as a flood: How is this possible? Maybe he can still recover. He's too young for this. It's not fair. How will his wife endure the loss? I'm not ready for our discussions to stop; why do they have to? I need more time with him. On and on these thoughts tumbled chaotically through his head. After a while, he forced his thoughts back to the present and prepared to leave.

About an hour later, he turned onto the street where his friend lived. Still deep in thought and almost oblivious to his location, he nearly drove past the house. Gathering himself together, he parked, walked to the door, and rang the doorbell. The living room was filled with people. Some had tear-filled eyes, others were hugging without speaking. He felt like an intruder, but everyone was gracious. He shared their feelings of grief. Someone quickly ushered him into the study. He was surprised at what he saw.

The older man was sitting in his customary chair, smiling. Seeing the tear-stained cheeks and lines of sadness on the face of his young friend, he said, "It will help me if you don't bring such a long face into my room. I'd appreciate it if you would go back into the hall and come back looking more cheerful."

Acknowledging the wisdom of the request, the young man stepped into the hall and thought about the many good things that had happened since he started visiting there. He thought of the good humor of his friend and remembered that happiness is a choice. Soon he was able to return to the study with normal color in his cheeks and a hint of a smile.

"Thank you. You look much better, and it makes me feel better. We have a lot to talk about today and can't spend time feeling sorry for ourselves."

The young man sat down on the comfortable leather couch, put his journal on the table, and let his friend's enthusiasm soothe him.

The older man continued talking, "Well, I thought I'd be talking with you about all this a little later, but now is a good time. First, I want to tell you about the gifts. Then I want to give you an assignment. I've already written what I am about to tell you, so you won't have to write while I'm speaking. Let me just dive in. I'm going to read some of this, so I won't leave anything out." Lifting several typewritten pages from the table, the older man began.

The Gifts

Centuries ago, in a far away land, a wise man began guiding others on their personal odysseys through the struggles and toils of life. Over the years, his reputation for wisdom grew, and many travelers came to him. In every case, the desire of the teacher was to help the traveler find the true way. He understood that well-chosen, powerful metaphors or symbols would greatly enhance the learning of his students. He also had learned by experience that when the use of powerful metaphors is accompanied by meditation and open conversation, the learning penetrates deeply, sometimes into the very soul of the student.

Knowing these things, the teacher searched widely for symbols that would help his students. Over a period time, he carefully selected unique objects to help guide his students. He called them gifts. The first gift was an hourglass to be used to help his students understand the meaning of time. The steady, consistent motion of the grains of sand encouraged his students to take time to think about the past, the present, and the future. As the second gift, he chose an elegant hand mirror to remind his students about their varied parts. He explained that, 'the heart, mind, and body make up all of the self.' And he had the inscription, 'What you see Is not all of me,' lightly engraved on the back of the mirror. I am told that he loved to see how long it would take a student to find the words.

The third gift was an well-crafted, mahogany box to remind his students that the Creator carefully chose what he placed in the space where we live. To assist his students, he sent each one on a journey similar to the one you experienced. When they returned, they usually understood that space is never empty. And they understood that the

Creator filled the empty space with his creations and then put his children in that space to allow them to learn how to find and follow truth and also how to serve others.

When he sent them to an unpopulated, wooded area similar to the meadow, he gave them a compass to use as their guide. Upon their return, they talked about the feelings they had experienced in the meadow. Over time, his students learned to recognize those feelings as spiritual promptings, guiding them along paths of truth. For thirty or forty years he succeeded in helping others, using these methods of powerful metaphors, or symbols, coupled with meditation and rich conversation.

Then one day, he realized that he would not live much longer. In all those years he had never let the objects leave his home. He had given his students similar gifts, but he kept the originals. About that same time, a new seeker came to him searching for answers. This student showed unusual understanding as the principles were unfolded to him. He quickly grasped the meaning of the gifts and applied them in his life. Shortly before his death, the teacher chose this student as his successor and presented him with the original gifts.

In time, the student became known far and wide for his wisdom and insightful guidance. Many came to him seeking his counsel. He followed the example of his teacher and used the gifts to help. He added yet another idea, one taught in an ancient record. In that story, a sage, a man of wisdom, discouraged by the events of his life, went into the mountains to escape his difficulties. While he was there, a great wind came and destroyed the rocks around him. After the wind came an earthquake, and after the earthquake a fire. In none of those cataclysmic events did the sage find God. Then came a still, small voice. The man of wisdom learned to listen to the still, small voice of God.

The successor taught his students that they could find the calm feelings of the still, small voice and take it with them as a compass to guide them to truth. He suggested that the compass could be a reminder of the still, small voice. In time, the successor passed the gifts and his experiences on to another student, one who showed special affinity for the message. He became the successor.

From the beginning until this day, this story has only been shared with those who receive the gifts. And now you, my young friend, have been chosen as protector of the gifts and the one to perpetuate the message. All who have the gifts have added wisdom to the story. And so shall you.

"Why me?" the young man asked incredulously. "I haven't even discovered the answers to my own questions. How can I ever be one to give counsel or help to others? Why would anyone listen to me when I've been such a dismal failure?"

"I wish I could answer those questions," his friend answered, "but I can't. In fact, I have wondered myself. But this I know: When you were a young boy growing up in your parents' home, you showed great promise. You were a child of influence among your peers. I thought of you even then as one who might receive the gifts. When you strayed, I believed the opportunity was lost for you. But when you came seeking answers, I watched you discover the meaning of the gifts more rapidly than any seeker had before. During this time, I felt it was to be you. When I learned of my illness shortly after your first visit, I was certain. How you will accomplish this mission or what you may add is yet to be seen. I can only say the gifts are yours; use them wisely. You should remember you did not choose the gifts. In effect, they chose you."

For a moment the young man was silent. Then he began questioning the choice again. "What am I to do with this? My life is filled with error. How can one like me help others? I don't know where to begin."

"Those are worthy and familiar questions. All successors had similar ones. None lived a life free of error, or they wouldn't have become students of the gifts. You're as qualified as any of the others. As you embark, we must cover one more subject. Up to now, all of our discussions have centered in ideas, not real actions. It is now time to change that, or you will fail.

"I'll use a simple illustration to make my point. When we hear a new idea or have a dose of inspiration, we often say, "Aha!" Or if it's a very good idea, we might say, "AHA!!" Sometimes for fun, I call the big AHAs, industrial strength AHAs. Then, when we apply an AHA in our lives and it works for us, we often say, "Wow." Or if it's really significant, we might have an industrial strength "WOW!" In the time we've been meeting, we've emphasized the discovery of ideas, the Aha's. But now, it's time for you to get out of the classroom, put these ideas into practice, and see them work in your life and in the lives of others. You need some wows and some WOWs with the principles we've been discussing."

Wanting to make sure the young man understood, the mentor added, "Let's use some of the gifts to emphasize the point: We're reminded by the symbol of the mirror that I must involve "all of me" in what I do. It's now time for you to involve your body by acting upon the things you have been learning, not just your heart and mind. We also learn from the symbol of the box that God placed others in this space. You must now reach out to others and use your gifts to help them. The mission associated with the gifts is: Act now, help others, and do so with God's influence."

At that moment, the host's daughter entered the room and announced that some out-of-town visitors had just arrived. The room soon flooded with others. To the young man, it was almost as if he disappeared. His dear friend squeezed his hand, bidding him farewell. Suddenly, he was standing outside, his mind filled with questions, and there was no one to ask.

He never saw his mentor alive again.

8

A New Beginning

Somehow the young man expected the day to be overcast and gloomy. Instead it was bright and sunny. The colorful fall leaves and crisp autumn air gave the impression of a time of celebration, not of sorrow or grief. The funeral service was much the same. The speakers, including family members, mentioned the highlights of a man's life filled with love of family, service to the community, and kindness to all. And the minister reminded everyone of the glorious resurrection and that all could expect to see this remarkable man in heaven's glory.

It was little consolation to the one who had received the legacy of the gifts. The words spoken in tribute to his mentor only seemed to highlight the young successor's weaknesses. As he left the service, he was confused and somewhat angry, though he didn't show it at the cemetery where hundreds of people gathered after the funeral to pay their final respects.

As everyone began to leave, he stepped over to the side, waiting. Soon, he saw the woman from the meadow making her way slowly toward him. "I'm glad you stayed," she said. "I really wanted to talk with you today."

"I hoped to see you, too. This has been a very difficult week. I wasn't ready to lose him."

She touched his shoulder without saying anything for a few minutes. Eventually, she broke the silence. "I know something about the history of the gifts, but nothing about their future. I wonder if you know what happened to them?"

"I didn't know it when we met in the meadow," he answered. "The hourglass you saw was the original. I have the other gifts, too. They're all sitting on a table in my apartment, hoping their rightful owner will arrive soon."

"What exactly does that mean?" she asked honestly. "Did you end up with them by accident? By some quirk of fate?"

Appreciating the opportunity to talk with someone, the successor explained. "Since our visit in the meadow, our friend and I have talked a lot about the gifts. He had assured me that the gifts were mine to keep. And the day before he passed away, he told me why."

The woman paused and didn't say anything for such a long time that it almost became uncomfortable. It was as if she had disappeared inside herself for a moment. As the light of recognition came into her eyes, she shook her head in a positive way. "So you're the successor. My, what a marvelous opportunity."

"Is that what it is? An opportunity?" He asked in a sarcastic tone. "It seems like nothing but a burden. And not only that, it's a burden I can't possibly carry. I have no experience helping others with problems, and my life to date hardly justifies anyone coming to me and asking for help."

"You're making a lot of assumptions that aren't true, my young friend," she rejoined. "I know something of the story and the power of the gifts, certainly not everything, but some things. I think if you truly understood the history, you'd feel honored, inadequate, but not abandoned or alone. Oh, there's my ride," she said, interrupting the train of thought. "This is probably timely. I suspect you're going to have to discover these things by yourself."

As she slowly walked away, the young man called after her, "I really enjoy talking with you. Do you suppose we could meet again?"

"Of course," the woman answered. "You know where I am almost every Saturday, just after dawn." And then she opened the door and blended into a mass of departing cars filled with people who were glad they had come to the funeral.

In no time, the cemetery was empty. The young man waited a distance away from the gravesite until the sexton and his crew finished and left. The fresh mound of earth was completely covered with bouquet after bouquet of flowers of almost every kind—impressive, visual symbols of the love and respect all had for the beloved man who was buried there. Echoes of tributes spoken in small groups seemed to ripple silently through the trees. Unfortunately, the young man had temporarily lost his ability to appreciate such things, he was so wrapped up in his own thoughts.

He stood alone, silently wishing for one last conversation. To him this was neither the time nor place for celebration of great memories; the setting was a symbol of a tragedy. The loss of his guide, his personal compass, was more than he was ready to bear. Just when he was beginning to see that his life had purpose and meaning, he had lost the narrator to his odyssey. Hardly lifting his head, he wandered along the narrow cemetery roads until he found his car. Looking at his watch, he remembered he had a lot to do that day and needed to hurry.

Stopping by his apartment for a late lunch, he immediately saw the blinking light of his answering machine as he walked through the door. Pushing the button while he hurried into the kitchen, he heard a familiar voice.

"Hey, Buv. It's me, your starving younger brother down at school. My roommates think I'm working out to become slim and trim. I'm reluctant to tell them my story:

no money, no food, no fat. Seriously, I'm hoping you'll be able to come down here soon. I'll make you rich when we set up the business. Call me when you can. Love ya."

The cheerful voice of his younger brother momentarily lifted his spirits. He promised himself he would call him that night. While he was quickly eating lunch, his thoughts returned to the loss of his mentor. The successor was learning that grief is a difficult taskmaster. Now that those emotions had started, he knew he would have a difficult time shaking his sadness. "But I still need to make it on time to this afternoon's appointment," he said to himself while he hurried out the door.

He didn't feel like selling anything, let alone making a pitch to a group of car salesmen. Although his life had become routine and predictable, he had recently started to enjoy it. This had been a good change in his mood and outlook. For months after his disastrous family experience, he had withdrawn from a more active business life. Before his personal problems ate away at his confidence and drive, he was a young man on a mission. However, since then he only wanted to make enough money to make ends meet, limiting his social life to immediate family and a few close friends. He just wanted to be alone to work through the results and consequences of his poor choices. In the meantime, he developed a simple product, a product to help car dealerships sell more cars. When he went to a dealership sales meeting, he was usually given five to ten minutes to make his presentation. Recently, his sales began to increase, which he attributed to "getting his pitch down."

An hour and a half after leaving the cemetery, he was sitting in the back of a sales room, waiting his turn. It came before he was ready. He was still lost in his troubled thoughts, but stood up quickly reaching into his memory for the familiar words to say.

"What would it take to increase sales here at this dealership?" he asked, using the question that had often worked before.

"Fire Brad, the service writer," said one, punctuating his comments with a derisive laugh.

Immediately, the group of fifteen broke into almost unanimous applause and the air was filled with a cacophony of sounds in support of the suggestion. "Yeah, fire him or shoot him," said another.

"Absolutely," said a third. "Why, with his rude blasts of anger toward customers, he's cost me more sales than I can count."

And so it went for the next few minutes. He lost control of the group before he had even begun his presentation. In fact, the sales manager took over, suggesting to the young man that he come back in two weeks when they would have time again. Even though he had been preoccupied when he stood in front of the group, he was confident about his product and his presentation. So he was unaffected by the turn of events and gratefully accepted the new appointment.

On his way out, his curiosity took him to the service area. He stood to the side and watched Brad, the service writer, as people came one at a time to his window. The line of people was always three or four deep and the young man could feel the intensity of the conversations, even from where he was standing. Soon, he decided to stand in line and meet the man who had engendered such animosity from the sales staff.

When he reached the front of the line, he stuck his hand through the large round hole in the glass. Introducing himself, he said, "Hi, I've just finished a meeting with the salespeople and I'd like to take you to lunch so we can talk about it."

"Oh, you've been meeting with the slicks, have you," the man behind the glass said in a tone filled with contempt. "Better you than me."

Then staring the young man straight in the eyes, he added, "Look Pal, I don't know what you're selling, but I ain't buying. Nor am I going to lunch with you. Look behind you, there are seven people in line ready to bite my head off. I don't need you telling me about the slicks. Get out of my line and leave me alone."

Undaunted, the young man responded. "I'm not selling anything, but I do want to take you to lunch. I'll be back in this area Tuesday; maybe that will be a better day. Besides, it won't cost you anything and I think I can help you." He was surprised at his own boldness, but he really believed he had valuable information to share.

However, without even looking up, the service writer bellowed, "Get out of my line and leave me alone. I'm not buying what you're not selling and I'm not going to lunch."

Unaffected by the response, the young man stepped aside, wrote a note to himself and left.

For the next several evenings, the young successor studied the gifts and wondered how he would ever be able to make use of them beyond the application to his own problems. He read his journal notes from his last meeting with his mentor, seeking clues that might be of help. He found a note that interested him.

The Compass: This has been a terrible day. I've lost my only real compass. For these past six months, I relied upon the guidance of my mentor to help me. I know he sent me to the meadow to learn to identify the feelings that tell me I'm headed in the right direction. And the compass is a reminder that I don't need a meadow; I can listen to an internal or still, small voice. That's not very helpful now. I'm sure I'll have to visit the meadow often to stay sensitive to those feelings. Maybe the still, small voice will come later. I hope so.

Soon, Tuesday came. It was late morning and the young man knew he'd have to rush. He arrived just before noon. Hurrying to the service department, he was relieved to see a line in front of Brad's window. He quickly got in the back, just before Brad's loud voice bellowed out to anyone who could hear.

"Whoever is at the end of the line right now, you're the last one before I go to lunch. I see four people. If anyone else comes, they're just out of luck"

Patiently, the last "customer" waited his turn. "I don't know if you remember me, but I promised to take you to lunch today. I keep my promises, so I'm here. Where would you like to go?"

Looking up and becoming immediately annoyed, Brad answered, "Look pal, I remember you. You're the one with the bad memory. I told you my feelings. I'm not buying anything and I'm not eating lunch with you. Now, get outta my line and outta my life!" With that he pulled the wooden curtain down and slammed it against the glass.

Moving quickly, the young man rushed to the side door just as Brad opened it. With a persuasive smile, he asked, "Where do you want to go to lunch? My car's right outside and the lunch is free."

"Promise me you aren't selling anything," Brad answered, somewhat reluctantly.

"I promise I'm only selling a free lunch."

"Okay," Brad answered. "But, I've only got forty minutes, then I have to be back here."

On the way over, Brad learned that his host graduated from high school the same year he did. In fact, they went to rival high schools in a city nearby. They even knew some of the same people. During the drive, the conversation became easier. They arrived at the restaurant in a few minutes. After walking through a short line, the two men placed their orders and found a table where they continued their discussion.

"Brad, I think you deserve a lot of credit for what you do," his new friend observed honestly.

"What do you mean?"

"I couldn't do what you do," he continued. "Why, I've watched you deal with a number of customers last week and today. They all had one thing in common. They had a complaint about their car and they took it out on you. Most of them were angry. I don't know how you do it."

Brad didn't say anything. His eyes started to mist up; he began to get a little emotional. His chin even started to quiver a little bit.

Trying to recover, the young man said, "Gee, I'm sorry, I didn't want to make you feel uncomfortable. I just think you deserve a lot of credit for what you do."

He seemed embarrassed. And so the successor tried to apologize again, but Brad resisted and said, "No, that's okay."

Just then they heard their order number called. The host said, "I'll go get it." When he returned, it was obvious that Brad had broken down. There were tear streaks on both cheeks.

"Brad, I'm sorry," the young man stated. "This wasn't my intention."

Neither defensive nor apologetic, Brad answered honestly. "No, it's just...uh...I know everybody at the dealership hates me. Frankly, I don't even like my job, but somebody has to do it. The slicks, they just don't get it. And in fact, no one has ever told me they appreciate what I do. Not a single person. Ever. Not in the five years I've been there."

"Well, I don't think you receive the credit you deserve," he affirmed again, "and I'm going to tell the sales force what I've seen today."

"It won't make a difference," Brad objected. "Those guys all hate me."

They finished their lunch talking about high school days and left the restaurant. About two weeks later, at the appointed time, the young man returned to the car dealership with clear intentions.

When it was his turn to make a presentation, he told the group about watching Brad's customers. He described the predictable anger most of the customers displayed and gave a sympathetic summary of his feelings that Brad carried an unusual burden for all of them.

"Oh, too bad," said one. "Brad attracts anger because he creates it. He's a carrier. I have no sympathy for that jerk. Brad is getting what he deserves."

"Yeah, let's stop the pity party for Brad," said another. "He cost me a sale just last week. That's bread off my table and food out of my family's mouth."

"Say," said a third, his tone of voice getting more upset with every word, "are you a psychologist, or are you here to sell us a product that will help us?"

At first the young man was distressed by the conflict he started, but he quickly recovered and made his sales presentation. As he drove away from the dealership, he shook his head. "Well, that just proves my point. I'm pretty good at selling this product, but I'm an abysmal failure when it comes to making a difference in someone's life."

That evening, the young man pulled his journal from the shelf and opened to a blank page.

There's not much of value to write today. I made a presentation at a dealership using all four of the gifts:

The Hourglass: I didn't wait for the future or worry about the past, I acted now, in the present, in my effort to help Brad the service writer.

The Mirror: I used all of me, heart, mind, and body, to prepare and present my ideas. I listened to Brad and spoke to the sales staff with my heart. The conversation and presentation were designed to appeal to the heart. I watched Brad's customers and analyzed their behavior with my mind. I prepared my presentation to the sales staff with my mind. I acted upon my observation— that's the body in action. It didn't matter.

<u>The Box</u>: In the "empty" space filled by God with self, others and His creations, I reached out to others, the sales staff, to show them how they could make a difference in their own lives and the life of another. It didn't matter.

<u>The Compass</u>: As I prepared to help Brad, I felt the calm, peaceful feelings like those I have felt in the meadow. It was like a reassurance that my efforts would be rewarded. It didn't matter.

What he didn't know was that while his comments to the sales staff fell on mostly deaf ears, one salesman who had his own reason to hate Brad, was listening carefully.

9

Rian's Story

The young man went to bed that evening more discouraged than ever. His efforts to follow in the footsteps of his mentor had failed. Perhaps a long night's rest would be good therapy, he thought as he fell asleep. In that hope he was disappointed as a ringing phone woke him up in the middle of the night.

"Hello," he responded groggily. He was immediately awake when he heard the news that his brother was missing. "When was he seen last?" he asked, anxiously.

"About ten o'clock," said the voice on the phone. "No one's heard from him since he left his apartment. He was supposed to be here before midnight, and it's after two-thirty now."

"What can I do?" the young man asked.

"Nothing now, but stay by the phone. We'll call you as soon as we've heard something."

The young man slowly hung up his phone. A tear trickled down his cheek as a profound sense of emptiness started in the pit of his stomach and gradually pushed out until it filled his chest. Almost numb, he walked over to the bookshelf and pulled out his journal. In the back he had put several moments of learning stories that were in various stages of completion. He found the one he wanted and began reading.

Outnumbered

I'm the oldest of nine children. After I was born, my parents had four daughters in a row. What are the odds of that happening? Well, in our family, it's one hundred percent. Now, don't misunderstand me. I love my sisters very much. My dad taught me that as the oldest and as a boy, I should always protect my little sisters. There were some exceptions, but most of the time things were good, and I followed Dad's counsel. I did grow up in a house filled with Barbie dolls and sometimes I found a training bra lying around the house. That was always a little embarrassing, especially if I had a buddy over and he noticed it first.

Suffice it to say, with all these girls around and me the only boy, I wanted a little brother in the worst way. My best friend, Blaine Wilhelm, lived across the street. He had an older brother named Steve. So, he always had a ready-made buddy—someone who could play ball or go to a John Wayne movie. Me, I usually watched Doris Day movies (chick flicks they call them today) or nothing at all. I really <u>needed</u> a little brother.

When Mom was pregnant with child number four, I asked, "Mom, how about a little brother this time?"

My mother responded with her most understanding voice, "Well, Son, I'd love to have another little boy, but I don't control that. You'll have to talk to your father."

When I went to Dad, he just rolled his eyes, as if to say, "Talk to your, Mom." I'd been in those round-robin loops before, bounced from one parent to the other. Sometimes I could figure out how to work one against the other. But this time it didn't help. After Dad rolled his eyes, I didn't bring it up to him again. In fact, he seemed as troubled as me. I think he wanted another boy, too.

A short time later, Mom went to the hospital and brought home another girl—JoDee—number three for those who are counting. JoDee was followed by my sister Jill. That made four sisters and me. By the time Mom was pregnant with number six, I was desperate. I really needed a little brother.

As the weeks passed, I tried every idea I could think of to help affect the outcome. I volunteered to do the dishes, set the table, vacuum, and keep my room clean. Mom accepted all offers, but made no guarantees. "All I can promise is that I'll do my best." That seemed okay at first, after all that's what she made me promise all the time. "Just do your best." But as the day for delivery grew closer, I increased my pleadings. "Please Mom, no more girls," was replaced with stronger words of encouragement. "Mom, I know you can have a boy. You had me."

When she answered with, "Remember, Son, I don't control that." I felt stymied. Somehow I knew Dad wasn't going to affect the outcome this late in the game.

The day she left for the hospital, I had a brainstorm. I rushed to the kitchen and announced, "Mom, I have the perfect solution. I've been thinking about it all week."

Now Mom rolled her eyes, but I was undaunted. "Dad told me that the room where the brand new babies are kept is filled with little girl babies and little boy babies. I'll bet when you go to the hospital for this baby, there's a family there just like ours, but different. They need a girl. So Mom, suppose you have another girl. What would you think of trading for a boy?"

Mom looked shocked and said, "We can't do that."

I said, "We can Mom, before we learn to love her. We wouldn't know the difference. And I'd have a little brother."

"I can't believe you'd even think of something like that, Son. Which one of your sisters would you give away for a little brother?"

"All of them, Mom." (I was only eleven years old at the time and it hadn't been a very good week with my sisters!)

Soon after that conversation, Mom went into labor and Dad took her to the hospital. My grandmother came over that morning to help get us off to school. About halfway through the school day I got a note from the principal's office. That always made me a little nervous. But when I opened the note, it said:

It's a boy.
Love,
Dad

As soon as I read it, I let out a whoop so loud I got sent to the principal's office.

That night when my dad came home he brought me a record. Remember that was before cassettes and CD's. It was a song by the Hollies and was called "He Ain't Heavy, He's My Brother." I played the song over and over again until my sisters hid if from me.

In those days, children weren't allowed to go to the hospital to see newborns. When I asked why, I was told that it was because children had germs. I wanted to get them surgically removed, but they wouldn't let me. So I had to wait three days for my little brother to come home.

Every night Dad would come home and say, "Oh, Son, wait until you see your little brother. He is so cute."

Finally, three days after my little brother was born, Dad and Mom brought him home. The day I met my baby brother Rian was one of those special times when words can't express feelings. But I can describe the event.

When the car drove up, I ran outside to open the door. Mom sat there for a moment, moving the blanket so I could see his tiny head, "Here's your little brother, Son."

"Can I hold him, Mom?" I asked, more excited than I'd ever been. It was even better than when I won the tetherball contest.

"Let's go inside first," she answered, while Dad peeled me off the seat.

Rushing inside, I hurried to the old English rocker and waited. Soon Mom came in and carefully put my little brother in my arms. She showed me how to hold him, how to support his back and his neck. Then she completely uncovered his face, and I looked at my little brother for the very first time. I knew I had seen his face before.

It really startled me. I looked at my parents and said, "Mom, I've seen this little baby before right in this room; you and Dad were standing there, too."

Mom said, "Son, that's impossible, he's home for the very first time."

I couldn't explain it, but I later concluded it was a gift to me, a gift that made my feelings for my little brother even stronger than they would have been. It was a good thing, too, but I'll explain that later.

Watching me and my new little brother Rian, my mom got a little emotional and said to my dad, "Oh, look, they're bonding."

It was more than bonding. The process of welding comes to mind. Anyway, that's how it all started. After years of pleading, failed deal making, saying both quick and long prayers, Rian finally came. It was just like I expected. In fact, it was even better. I was there to help. I read to him, fed him, and generally assisted in every way I could think of. When he was eleven months old, I was the one who taught him how to walk. And when he got older, I took him everywhere. I'd go out to play with my friends and say, "Mom, I'm taking Rian with me."

She'd often say, "Oh, you don't have to take him everywhere."

"That's okay, Mom, he ain't heavy, he's my brother. I didn't sing it, and I think my sisters were glad 'cause I couldn't sing well. They gave me a hard time every time I even said, "He ain't heavy, he's my brother." I didn't care.

My friends made fun of me. "Why do you always have to watch your little brother? You got all those sisters at home, but you always have to watch him. How come?"

"What do you mean watch him," I'd say. Then it dawned on me. "Oh, you thought I brought him because I had to watch him. Nah, that's not why I brought him. I brought him because I want him with us. Do you know how long I waited for this little guy? And to make it better, he's a cool kid. I just want him with us."

They'd say, "But he'll just get in the way."

"Well, then, you guys go do whatever you want," I'd say. "I'm going to do something with Rian."

Even today I don't fully understand why I was this close to my little brother. But I can say that when I got into high school, I still took him everywhere. I'd go to high school football and basketball games, and I'd take my little brother. Everybody took a date. I took my little brother. (And we had a better time.)

I even took him on some of my dates. One night I had a date with Donna Compton. We were going to a movie. As we came out of her house, I opened the car door for her. By the time I was behind the wheel, she'd turned around and discovered Rian in the back seat.

He said, "Hi, Donna."

She was confused. "What is he doing here?" she asked. "Are we dropping him off somewhere?"

"No," I said. "He wants to see the movie we're going to see. I thought I'd bring him with us."

"You're bringing your brother on a date?"

"I know, isn't that a cool idea?" I turned around and gave Rian a thumbs up and he gave me a thumbs up, too. I can't speak for Donna, but Rian and I had a great time.

While I was in high school, I only weighed ninety-eight pounds, but still made the wrestling team. My nickname was Thunder Guppy. Rian came to every one of my wrestling matches. I'd always be the first one to wrestle. I'd get out in the middle of the mat and signal Rian with a thumbs up and then I'd make a fist and raise it high in the air. He'd give me the same thumbs up and then he'd make a fist and raise it high. To us, these signals had special meanings. Be strong. Win the match. Go for the pin. When my teammates asked what I was doing, I told them it was good luck and that I always won when Rian was there and we made those signals. They started signaling Rian, too.

"Hey, it worked," they'd say. "I won my match. He is good luck."

I said, "Yeah. I told you."

"Bring him again next week."

"Oh," I said, "He comes to every match. He's my little brother. I take him everywhere."

When he came to this point in the story, which was as much as he had written, he picked up the phone and called his parents. "I can't stand the waiting. I'm going to get some things together and come on out to your place."

He was in his parents home when the phone rang. His father picked it up. "It's the highway patrol," he said to those gathered in the living room, waiting. "Yes, sir. Thank you. We'll leave for the hospital right now." Hanging up the phone, he turned to the group. "Rian's in an ambulance on the way to the hospital. A truck driver lost control and crossed over into Rian's lane. The impact drove both of them off the road. No one saw the car until about thirty minutes ago. It doesn't look good. Rian was thrown through the windshield. We'd better go."

For three days, the family waited, hoping for a miracle. Finally, the father gathered all the family members into Rian's room. He was on life support. They were faced with the awful decision of ending his life. Taking Rian's hand in his, the father asked everyone to join hands. The young man stood on the other side of the bed, taking Rian's other hand in his and grasping the hand of one of his sisters. His father looked across the room at the young man.

"Son, I'm so sorry. I know how much you'll miss him. We'll all miss him. He was a son and a brother to us all, but he was your best friend. I'm not sure I can fully understand the void this will leave for you, especially during this difficult time in your life."

In a few minutes, Rian was removed from life support and was pronounced dead a short time later. At the funeral, a roommate of Rian's approached the young man with an envelope in his hand. "I found this stuck in Rian's mirror. It had your name on it. So I brought it today. I thought you'd want it."

Although he wanted to read it immediately, he waited until he was in his apartment. He opened the envelope and found a birthday card with a letter in it.

Dear Buv,
I'm really proud of myself. I bought your birthday card a week early. I wanted time to write some of the things in my heart. As far back as I can remember, you've been there for me. I don't know what I did to deserve it, but I have the best brother on the planet. This past week, when you came down to teach me the business, I was reminded once again what a great guy you are. After we went to four car dealerships and

sold them all and you gave me the commissions even though you sold three of them, I couldn't believe it, but I shouldn't have been surprised. I told a friend what you said when I resisted—payment for helping you win all those wrestling matches. He couldn't believe it either.

I'm so sorry about the death of your mentor. It sounds like he was one in a million. He couldn't be any more remarkable than you. While he responded whenever you called, you've always searched for opportunities to help me. That's even better. You're a natural helper.

When I think of the gifts he gave you, I can see why he thought you'd be the perfect successor. An hourglass could be your trademark. There's no one who understands time like you do. You've always found time for me and for lots of others. And as for the mirror, well, I've often told Mom that you put all of yourself into whatever you do. My motto has been "leave it all on the field." I learned that from you. We give our all or it's worth nothing. That's what you've always said. That's heart, mind, and body, even though we never called it that. As for the space in the box, it seems to me that there is a balance between the three things in the box, self, others, and God's creations. But if one is out of balance, it's probably best to favor others. You're great at that. Remember all those Christmases when we did secret Santa, just the two of us. What a lesson for a little brother fixed on getting stuff for Christmas. I know you feel like you lost your compass for a while, but you've found it now, and with this new opportunity as keeper of the gifts, you'll never lose your way again.

As you can tell, I think you're the perfect choice as successor. You've been doing it all your life. By the way, I bet if you go back and check on that Brad guy, the service writer, something good has happened to him. And whenever you doubt your talent for helping others, imagine you see a thumbs-up and my fist raised in the air. Remember what it means: Be strong. Win the match. Go for the pin. You're the best!

  Love you always Buv,
   Rian

Tears were streaming down the face of the young man as he picked up the phone. After gathering himself together he dialed a number. "Service department, please."

"Brad here, how can I help you?" said the cheerful voice on the end of the line.

Startled at the tone, the young man identified himself. Before he could say anything else, Brad broke in. "It's great to hear from you. Some good things have happened since you were here. But I'd rather tell you in person. Can we go to lunch tomorrow?"

The next day, as soon as he saw the young man, Brad came out from behind the counter. "Let me show you something," he began. Walking over to a display case, Brad showed him the plaque for salesman of the month. It said Pete Mauritsen.

"Look carefully," Brad added.

Engraved below Pete's name was Brad Wilson, Service Manager. "How did this happen?" the young man asked, very interested.

"I want Pete to tell you. Here he comes now." After introductions were made, Brad suggested that they eat in the company lunchroom. "The food's not that great, but we need to return to the scene of the crime." Both Brad and Pete laughed at the comment, promising to explain later.

After they sat down, Brad suggested that Pete tell the story. "After all, you're the hero here."

"Well, I don't know about being a hero, but something good has happened." Looking at the young man, he continued, "It was after you told your story in the sales meeting about having lunch with Brad. The story rang true for me because I know something about not being appreciated."

Pointing to his missing left arm, he explained that he lost it in Vietnam. "When I came home from the war, I expected to be a hero. Nothing could have been further from the truth. And the missing arm was an ugly reminder of a controversial war. I finally quit being honest about how it happened because, instead of the expected appreciation, I received disdain. When you said Brad deserved a lot of appreciation, and then reminded us that we gave him none, I determined right then to do something about it. Even though Brad and I had almost gotten into a fist fight right here in the lunchroom over his treatment of one of my customers, which ended in a lost sale, I decided to show a little appreciation.

"First, I went to Brad and apologized."

Interrupting, Brad said, "I didn't know how to accept it at first, but before we knew it, we'd become friends."

"And then," Pete said, "whenever one of my customers had a problem, Brad gave them first class treatment. Why, he'd even bring them to the front of the line, if necessary, or he'd make special note of their paperwork, making sure it didn't get lost. I began getting referrals from my customers. Needless to say, before two months had passed, I had sold more cars than ever before, more than anyone in the company. A lot of the guys got mad, but we didn't care. Some others are starting to see what's happened and have followed suit. Things are getting better around here. And it's all because of you."

After lunch, the young man went back to his apartment. There in the middle of the table was the card from Rian. Looking at the card, the young man made a thumbs up and then raised a fist in the air.

"It looks like we won another match, Rian. And I think we're on a roll."

10

Getting the Picture

The years passed. The young man grew older and life changed little by little. Eventually, he married again and became the father of two children. By the time his oldest child was fifteen, he had spent thousands of hours helping others, using the wisdom of the gifts. He had become an able successor to the mentor he so admired. However, he wondered if he would ever have anything to add, any wisdom of his own to pass along to the one who would succeed him.

He had taken a job in industry, working long hours to provide for his family and prepare for the future. Late one Friday afternoon he was looking forward to spending a free weekend with his family when his plans were unexpectedly interrupted.

"Would you come in here right now?" a voice boomed through the intercom into his office.

"What now?" he muttered as he slowly got up from his desk and walked to his manager's office, rolling his eyes as he went.

"Deadlines, deadlines, deadlines. That's all we ever hear," he complained as he returned to his office ten minutes later. Noticing his staff gathered around in anticipation, he added, "It's Friday, and Randy wants a new report on Monday."

As he parceled out the weekend assignments, he made sure he got the biggest part. "At least we can do this at home," one commented, while the others took their assignments with unintelligible grumbles.

Another looked at the team leader sympathetically, and hinted, "You shouldn't take so much on yourself. Isn't tomorrow the finals of your son's soccer tournament?" The comment apparently fell on deaf ears, as no one extended an offer of help. Actually, the team leader felt guilty about asking his people to take any work home on the weekend, especially when he knew that with better planning on his boss's part, there wouldn't be such a crisis.

An hour later, in a very foul mood, the successor left the parking garage and headed home, not relishing the thought of the Friday night traffic. His negative expectations were quickly realized as he met a seemingly endless array of drivers suffering from various stages of acute road rage. The final straw came as traffic slowed to a halt at an accident site because of rubbernecking motorists. The delay cost him at least thirty minutes of extra travel time, during which his frustration became even worse when he had to turn off his air conditioner to avoid overheating the engine in the sweltering summer heat.

At long last, he turned onto his street. Every muscle in his body was taut and tense. Pulling into the driveway, he slammed on the brakes to avoid missing a bicycle carelessly left in front of the garage. Muttering under his breath while shutting off the engine, he reached across the seat, grabbed his heavy briefcase, and got out. Frustrated, hot, and very angry about the situation at work, he stormed through the front door, hardly noticing the blast of cool air that greeted him as he marched through the entryway to the stairs. "Carl, come down here, right now!" he bellowed, waiting impatiently for the ten year old to appear.

Hearing his dad's voice and not accurately interpreting the tone, Carl bolted from his room carrying his soccer ball. Dad had promised to help him on his footwork for tomorrow's championship game, and Carl was excited to get started. Before he hit the first step, however, his father's angry voice almost reduced the lad to tears.

"I've told you a million times to put your bike away. Get out there and move it, or next time I'll just run over it."

Without noticing his son's confused and crestfallen look, he turned toward the kitchen. It was already six o'clock. He was hungry and tired. Puzzled that there were no hints of dinner in sight, he glanced around the room. Through the sliding glass doors he could see his wife, Connie, sitting at the edge of the pool, feet in the water, talking on the phone.

"It's been a great day," Connie said pleasantly into the phone. Unaware of the angry stare from the kitchen, she continued, "We raised $1,400 for the scout troop from local companies. It took all day, and I'm here soaking my tired feet, but I can't wait to tell him. He'll be so pleased. He told me when he left for work this morning that he was sure I could do this."

Unwilling to wait any longer, the frustrated husband marched across the kitchen, almost jerked the door off its track, and immediately confronted his celebrating wife. "Good grief, Connie," he said abruptly, "here it is Friday night at six, I'm exhausted, and supper's not even started. And where are you? Sitting at the edge of the pool, visiting with friends!"

Excusing herself, Connie quickly put down the phone and directed her entire attention to the cause of the interruption. "Honey, supper is not an entitlement. It's a gift. You have no right to demand it." Too disappointed to remind him that he had promised to take her out that night if she met her goal, Connie pushed her way past him, stomped through the kitchen while looking back at him. "As far as I'm concerned, you can fix your own dinner or go buy it somewhere else and eat it alone."

"That's fine by me," he responded angrily, struggling to understand why everyone was acting strange. He worked hard, but no one appreciated it.

At that moment his teenage daughter, Marie, slipped into the kitchen, wrestling with the exact way to form the sentence she had been working on all afternoon. "Uh, Dad," she stammered, remembering her mother's exact words: *"Dad always understands. He'll let you go."*

"Uh, Dad," she repeated anxiously.

Hardly even noticing her arrival, he didn't answer the first time. The second time she spoke, he was still trying to sort through all that had happened since he got home, his continuing frustration apparent. "What is it now, Marie," he growled.

Having worked her courage up for this moment, Marie continued, "Uh, the prom is only four days before my sixteenth birthday. Tim Mason invited me today. And, uh, Mom said to ask you if I could go."

"Not a chance," he countered, without listening. "A rule's a rule. They won't let you drive four days early. And the family rule about no dating before age sixteen won't be compromised either! What's happening around here? It seems like everything's falling apart." Turning on his heel, he walked to the family room and plopped down on the sofa.

Absentmindedly looking for something to take his mind off his frustrations, he picked up the family photo album. He opened the first page. He hardly noticed how beautiful Connie looked and how radiant they both were on their wedding day. Pushing that page aside, he slowly glanced through baby pictures, birthdays, and outings. By the time he reached their last summer vacation, his attention was fully fixed on the photos. He didn't even notice that his breathing had slowed and his anger was oozing away.

Pausing at the pictures from Disney World he grinned at the sight of the four of them in the log ride splashing into the water while clowning for the camera. He remembered how his determination to stand up almost resulted in a plunge in the water for him and Marie. The smile changed to a chuckle and then to a laugh just as Carl entered the room.

Seeing the obvious change in his father's attitude increased Carl's confidence. "What're you laughing at Dad?" his son asked with only a hint of caution.

"Carl, come and take a look at this."

In moments, father and son were reminiscing about a great summer vacation to Disney World, as they looked through several pages of colorful pictures. "Remember when the waiter dropped the tray, and the food landed in your lap, Dad?" Carl asked, bringing a smile to both their faces.

Hearing all the commotion and fearing the worst, Marie listened carefully from the upstairs where she had retreated only a few moments before. She stuck her head cautiously over the guardrail to check out the climate. Disarmed by hearing real laughter, she crept down the stairs and peeked around the corner. She was quickly invited to participate. Soon, she too, was remembering the fun of the summer. Her favorite part was sampling food from all over the world at Epcot Center. She reminded everyone of the time Mom tried to order Italian food from a "real Italian" and blew all the pronunciation, even though she had "taken two semesters of Italian in college." In the confusion, a pasta dish was brought for dessert.

Sensing that her father was back to normal, Marie called out to the master bedroom, "Hey Mom, you need to come here." Hearing no answer, Marie ran down the hall to the bedroom. "Come on, Mom, things have really calmed down. Please come and join us."

Still stinging from her husband's thoughtless rebuke, Connie only reluctantly allowed herself to be dragged down the hall by her bubbly daughter. When she saw the honest fun, she filed her feelings away for future reference, not quite willing to completely let them go.

Marie took the album from her dad and turned it to the picture of the Italian Restaurant. In the picture, the four of them were standing in front of the eatery holding a big plate of "pasta dessert."

"Remember this, Mom?" Marie said gleefully.

"I have to admit, I felt a little foolish," Connie agreed sheepishly, "though I have been tempted to invent a pasta dessert to cover my language goof!"

And so it went for another hour or so—page by page, minute by minute, remembering, laughing, teasing, and hugging. Out of nowhere, the ever-starving Carl interjected, "All this talk about food has really made me hungry, Mom. What's for supper?"

"Oh, I don't know," his mother answered pleasantly. "Let's go see what we can put in the microwave." Not breaking the spell, the two of them walked into the kitchen.

Dad and Marie continued talking until the phone rang. It was for Marie, and she left with a promise, "I'll be right back, Dad. Don't go away."

As suddenly as it had begun, the moment passed, but the mood lingered. Left alone, the successor wondered about how this had all come about. More importantly, he thought about his anger and his unkind comments to his family. Stunned by his own behavior, he admitted that he sometimes treated total strangers better than he treated his own precious family. He was, he acknowledged, embarrassed about how he had acted. Realizing he didn't feel even a tiny remnant of his bad feelings, he reconstructed the events that calmed him down. His eyes came to rest again on the family photo album. He picked it up and thumbed silently through the pages. This time he stopped at the first page, remembering his feelings about Connie on the day of their wedding. A tear formed in the corner of his eye as his mind skimmed through a mental photo album of their lives together—he remembered her support, her sacrifices, and her constancy.

"I can't let the pressures from work cause me to do such thoughtless things to them," he said out loud resolutely. "Otherwise, what's the point of working?"

Then the light went on. He picked up the photo album, tucked it under his arm and walked out to his car. Opening the passenger-side front door, he slid the album under the seat and made a commitment to himself that every night before he walked into the house, he would take time to look through the album. Then, having finished that project, he walked back into the house with a skip in his step, heading for the kitchen. Sticking his head just around the corner, he called out, "Hey, Little Girl, whatcha doing?"

Hearing the familiar term of endearment and still enjoying the mood created in the family room, Connie was an easy mark for a clearly repentant husband. "Well," she said with a calculated smile, "I'm not making supper for a grumpy husband, only for his two thoughtful children and myself."

"What if I promise to do the dishes for a week?" the negotiator asked.

"That's really not enough, but it's a good start," his wife answered with that smile that made him melt.

Later in the evening in the quiet of his study, he pulled his journal from the shelf.

I wonder if the moments of learning will ever stop coming. I've been a bear at work and at home. There is something magical about tonight's discovery. I think it'll be fun to examine tonight's events with the help of the ancient gifts.

The Hourglass: Here's a question I'm going to ponder for a few days: By using the photo album, what did I do to my understanding of the past that caused such a dramatic change in my feelings and behavior in the present? Maybe I've actually found that place where the past and present meet. Have I brought them together in some mysterious way? Or maybe I should just go to bed and quit thinking about this until another time. There is some intriguing idea here, though, that pleasant images of the past can have such a dramatic effect on the present. And for me, they'll do so for a long time.

<u>The Mirror:</u> I continue to explore the relationship between my thoughts, my emotions, and my actions. I have to keep all of me—heart, mind, and body—in balance in order to be the person I want to be. It ain't easy, but I'll keep working at it. I was amazed how easily my anger went away because of pictures of happy times. I mean, I really felt the mood shift, like a wave rushing through my body. That's a critical reminder of how much influence I have over my feelings. I must remember—happiness is a choice.

A few weeks later, he added a related thought.

There has been a ripple effect from the photo album night. People at work tell me my attitude has changed for the better. I'm more pleasant, they say. Imagine, someone with such an even disposition as me, showing improvement! Hah, hah. It's a good reminder that I need to be more sensitive to the people who matter the most in my life; my family, of course, but also people at work. As I've told the photo album story to some of those with whom I've shared the gifts, they've started using their own photo albums in similar ways, and it's worked for them, too.

From a simple event, the foundation for a significant idea was built. The best was yet to come.

11

Discovering the Rule

In spite of the positive effects of his use of the photo album, the life of the young successor continued to be filled with difficult time demands. As he became better known for his wise counsel about self improvement, he was frequently asked to speak on related subjects. At first he spoke to small groups in nearby locations, then he was transferred to the human relations and training department of his company, and he flew all over the county working to help others. Even though he worked hard to align his personal behavior with the principles he taught, he continued to see the gap between what he believed and taught and how he actually lived. At times his discomfort was almost palpable. A four-hour return flight from Los Angeles provided a typical example.

The plane was cruising high above the clouds and he was dozing when the man in the next seat broke up his reverie. "Hey, did you see this? Here's an article about how much time we spend with our families. Who writes this stuff? Someone without enough to do, I'd say." Then, putting the magazine in the seat back pouch, he added, "I don't need a guilt trip sponsored by someone I don't even know."

"Do you mind if I look at that?"

"Be my guest. If you want to suffer needlessly, go ahead."

Taking the magazine from his neighbor, he began to read carefully. He jotted a few notes in his journal for future reference.

A recent survey showed that the average father spends less than seven minutes a week in one-on-one, individual conversations with his children. In order to qualify, the conversations had to be held in normal tones of voice. Imagine that. I wonder if it's true for me. The guy in the next seat thought it was bunk.

I'll jot down a ledger for last week.

	Mon	Tue	Wed	Thur	Fri	Sat	Sun
Marie	0	0	0	0	8	0	0
Carl	0	5	0	0	0	0	0

He increased his ledger to include the previous four weeks. To his dismay, he learned that he averaged less than ten minutes a week with each child. He learned from the same survey that the average husband spends twenty-seven minutes a week in calm, one-on-one, private conversations with his wife. Creating another spreadsheet, he found that he averaged about thirty minutes a week in similar conversations with his wife. At first he was disappointed with himself. Then, gradually, as he thought about the significance of what he had learned, he was profoundly affected by his discoveries. His mind was whirling and his thoughts were racing as he considered the implications of this discovery.

In his journal he wrote:

I'm not sure anything like this has ever happened to me. The word epiphany comes to mind. [He left a blank space where he later wrote a definition.] *Epiphany: a sudden, intuitive perception of or insight into the reality or essential meaning of something, usually initiated by some homely or commonplace occurrence or experience.*

It's as if my whole life has been preparing me for this moment! In the shadow of the gifts, I can see events of my life as if they happened yesterday, and I see their meaning with a new perspective: The day of the tetherball game:

You can do anything for one minute. Meeting with my mentor and learning from his wisdom: Some things are true whether you believe them or not. Meeting the woman in the meadow: Search your life for the moments of learning. Happiness is a choice. The story that my mentor shared about attempting to feed his daughter spinach: What Do I control? Only my behavior. The loss of my brother Rian: I have to take advantage of every precious moment with those I love. The photo album: Families are too important to bring my frustrations home to them. Kindness is a choice.

My thoughts cannot be fully expressed in words. There is so much more to what I am feeling. But now I know what I have to do as a teacher, and what I can contribute to the legacy of the gifts. But first, I need to experience it for myself.

When the plane landed, he felt a calm enthusiasm. He was ready. And, in the spirit of his epiphany, he knew it wouldn't be some grand scheme, but a simple ordinary experiment. It was late, and he went home determined, but very tired. Everyone was asleep. Nevertheless, he took his photo album out from under the seat and sat in the living room for few minutes, turning the pages to remind him how much he loved his family. Then, relieved he could wait until next day when he had rested to start his experiment, he collapsed into bed, exhausted.

When morning came, he wondered if he had overreacted to the experience on the plane. Rereading his journal helped him regain his enthusiasm for the task. Looking at his watch, he realized that both of his children had already left for school, and he was running a little late for work.

"I'll catch them tonight," he thought as he raced out the door without breakfast.

On the way home, he remembered his commitment to himself and entered his home confidently. Seeing his wife in the kitchen, he called out, "Say, Honey, have you seen the kids?"

"Carl is spending the night at Ron's, and Marie's next door studying with some friends. She has a big test next week, and wants to do well. She'll be late."

Undaunted, he kept his spirits up, but had to wait two more days before everyone's schedule meshed. Finally, he came home and saw Carl across the street with some friends, riding his skateboard down the driveway.

In his most pleasant voice, he called, "Hey, Guy, got a minute?"

"Sure Dad, what's up?" Carl replied as he rolled back across the street, wondering if he was in trouble.

"Son, have I ever told you it was my generation that invented skateboards?"

Carl looked puzzled. "What do you mean, Dad?"

"Well, they didn't cost $197 like yours. We took our old steel roller skates apart and nailed them on the bottom of a two-by-four."

"Dad, how come you've never told me this before?"

"Oh, I'm sure I did, Son; you probably don't remember."

"No, Dad. I would've remembered. I love skateboards."

So he told his son about the games he played with his skateboard. He explained how he and his friends pretended they were in the Olympics by creating a difficult course and timing each other with a stopwatch. Whoever had the best time out of two runs got to keep the trophy in their bedroom window for a whole week—until the next Saturday.

"What a great idea, Dad. Do you have anymore stories?"

The two of them sat on the curb and talked for another twenty minutes before Carl went back to play with his friends. As he stood up to leave, his father said, "I'm about to initiate a new rule in the family, and I'm going to call it Dad's Rule."

"What's Dad's Rule?" The boy asked cautiously, thinking about more chores.

"It's a rule for Dads. For this Dad it means take five minutes every day and spend it with the people you love the most. It means telling skateboard stories and stuff like that."

"Five minutes isn't much time, Dad."

"It isn't. But believe it or not, it's more than I've been spending."

"Sounds good to me. I love your stories, Dad." And then he pushed his skateboard in front of him, hopped on, and skated off to join his friends.

As he watched his son skating across the street, a lump formed in the father's throat. Suddenly, tears streamed down his face. When his son turned around and saw him wiping tears away, he ran back across the street and gave him a hug.

"It's okay, Dad," he said with a grin. "I'm just going across the street. I'll be back for supper. I promise."

As Carl returned to his friends, his father renewed his determination; "That was great. Marie's next."

Returning to the house, he went upstairs and knocked on her door and said, "Marie, let's go for a walk." He knew he had to get her away from the telephone and her homework. "I want to talk to you. "

"What's the matter, Dad?"

"Nothing's the matter. I'm just very happy about what's going to happen."

They walked slowly around the block, talking all the way. It took them about fifteen minutes. When they got back to the front door, she said, "Dad, did Mom talk to you?"

"No, Princess, she didn't, at least not today."

"Then, Dad, we need to talk about something."

They walked around the block three more times. During the trip, a father learned more about his daughter in forty-five minutes than he had in the previous forty-five days. Later that evening, he wrote:

I know I'm on to something. The experiment worked great. This could be my legacy with the gifts. Carl and Marie were receptive to the approach. When I first explained to Connie what I was doing, she thought I was overreacting to the survey, but when she heard how the kids reacted, she asked to be on my list. I've decided to change the name of the rule to The Five-Minute Rule. Here's the rule: Spend five minutes every day one-on-one with each person who is important in your life, including those at home and at work. Talk to them in person or on the telephone. It's not that hard to spend five minutes every day alone with each member of your family to tell them that you love them and why. In order to do so, you must constantly be looking for the good things they do. The key is to tell them why you love and appreciate them. Also, it is not difficult to tell your coworkers how much you appreciate them and why they are important in your life. So just do it!

12

The Five-Minute Rule

A bitterly cold wind pushed against the young woman as she wearily made her way through the gate and up the long driveway. Tired from the two-hour drive and a long day at work, she was also apprehensive about telling anyone of the embarrassing problems she was facing. Only her father's assurance about the wisdom and experience of their family friend gave her confidence enough to face the challenge. Standing in the enclosed porch, she reconsidered one last time before pressing the doorbell. Even though she had called ahead to make an appointment, she nearly turned back, but the outside light came on and the door opened.

"Is someone there?" asked the kind voice of the older gentleman.

"Why, yes it's me," she answered, wiping a tear from her cheek. "And frankly, I'm not sure if I should be here. My dad suggested it."

"Well, why don't you come in, warm yourself a little, and then you can decide whether you should stay," the host suggested, opening the storm door for encouragement. Calling out to the kitchen, he asked, "Honey, do we have a little hot chocolate for a weary and chilled traveler? I think she needs a little thawing out."

By the time her coat was in the hallway closet and the young woman was seated comfortably in her host's library, a cup of steaming hot chocolate was sitting on a side table.

"How's your father enjoying retirement?" he inquired, his words heightening her sense of being in a safe place.

"Actually, he loves it. I don't know what I'd do if he and Mom weren't over at the house almost everyday, though I never thought we'd get him out of the dealership. He still gets calls every day from someone seeking his advice about something. After twenty-seven years, he knows so much about how things work there. By the time he retired, he had worked in almost every department."

"It's quite a story," her host mused, "and a remarkable career path, from service writer to general manager. I continue to hear reports that everyone loved to work for him. The new general manager says it's tough to follow the old pro. Just shows what one man can do when he sets his mind to it."

Gradually, her nearly frozen body thawed out, and she began to relax. "It's just like Dad said," she thought. "This man can make anyone comfortable."

"Just wait," he had encouraged, "you'll be talking his leg off before the hot chocolate cools."

Feeling more comfortable, the young woman began to share her story. "Seventeen years ago, I married a wonderful man. He was filled with energy and ambition. In time we were blessed with three very special children. Then as you know, four years ago, my husband was brutally murdered in a robbery late one evening as he was leaving his office. Since then my life has been anything but serene. My emotions range from bitterness, to anger, to an emptiness that is overwhelming. Rarely, if ever, do I even cross the path of happiness that I once knew, and it's not my fault. My life has been stolen from me. Sometimes I feel I have been dropped into the middle of someone else's life.

"Now, my older children are teenagers and becoming very difficult. My daughter, a beautiful sixteen year old,

94

has been mad at God since her father died. To use the modern term, she acts out her anger in totally inappropriate ways. I wish I could say that I am the model of control when I talk with her, but lately, as I've gotten more and more frustrated, I just lose it. My son, a handsome fourteen year old, is drifting away from me, too. He's running with a tough crowd and sees little value in my counsel. Unfortunately, he's been the victim of my outbursts as well. My youngest child, who just turned eight, has been a joy since the day he came home from the hospital. But I know that if I don't change something soon, he'll follow in the footsteps of his siblings and slip away from me just like they are."

Her host said very little as she continued her story. He listened intently, asking an occasional question. His sympathetic tone was a balm to the young woman, allowing her to be open and frank.

And so it was that a young woman filled with despair found a guide in the midst of her life's most difficult challenge. After spending thirty minutes telling her story, the host began to slowly describe a possible plan to help resolve her pain and difficulty.

Asking her to come with him, they went into a small study. In the corner of the room was a specially-designed crystal étagère with five individual shelves. A single object was carefully positioned on each shelf. A closer look revealed the heirloom quality of each one. "A long time ago," the host began, "a friend of mine gave me these treasures. I was a seeker with questions not so different from yours. My friend told me I would find the answers to my questions by studying these gifts. It took a long time to uncover the meaning behind each one. In fact, I think I'm still learning, but they have enriched my life immeasurably."

Gently opening the glass door, he took an hourglass from the top shelf and handed it to the young woman, inviting her to sit down at the same time. "Please turn it over and tell me what you see," he said kindly.

Placing the hourglass on the table between them, the host waited as the young woman took her time in answering. Because of her father, she knew something of her host's teaching methods. Surprisingly, she thought, she felt no pressure from her host, only encouragement.

After watching the motion of the sand for several minutes, she began to speak. "I see time passing slowly though the hourglass. Somehow I see my children in the hourglass. As much as time passes slowly, it is relentless, just like the growth of my children. This reminds me that I have to pay attention to them now." Then another wave of recognition crossed her face, "Oh! I see three compartments! I never thought of an hourglass as having three separate compartments! That's interesting. That's what I see. What do you see?" she asked honestly.

"I see a bright and capable young woman with some very difficult challenges," the older man began. "Tonight, if you choose to, you are about to begin a journey, an odyssey if you will, that will not only help you resolve the difficulties you face, but will serve as a guide throughout the rest of your life."

Then reaching into a wall cabinet, the host lifted a small box and handed it to her. "This is a gift from me to you," he explained. "Please open it."

She smiled as she lifted a well-crafted replica of the hourglass from the package. "Thank you. You're being very patient. My father told me you were a great teacher. He said if you were willing to work with me, you would help me gain control of my life. I'm here to learn."

"I can see that you are. If you spend time studying the hourglass, I think you'll discover some very useful insights. Normally, I would send you out tonight with your hourglass and the assignment to continue looking at it until you see what I can see. But my normal approach won't work in your situation."

"What do you mean?" she asked, her disappointment acute

"Don't you worry," he responded. "This will still work out. We'll just make some minor adjustments. As a general rule, I have my students meet here at my home regularly for several weeks, even months. During that time, I give them only one gift at a time. I don't think that approach will work well for you. Living more than two hours away is a challenge in itself, not to mention the time demands of three children and a full-time job. So I'm going to do this a little differently tonight. Then we can meet by phone when we need to. We'll just speed this up a little tonight and take our time later.

Stepping back to the étagère, he opened the door and withdrew an impressively decorated hand mirror. Handing it to the young woman, he asked, "Please tell me what you see."

Turning it over several times in the somewhat dim lighting, then looking at her reflection, she answered. "I see a jewel-studded hand mirror of the finest workmanship. I also see engraving on the back, which seems to be almost hidden. I think the engraving says, 'What you see is not all of me.' And I see my reflection surrounded by expensive jewels. I'm not sure how this relates to my circumstances, but that's what I see."

"Excellent," her friend responded, removing another package from the cabinet. "I have a similar hand mirror for you to study at home."

Then, stepping back to the étagère, he carefully selected two other items and placed them in front of her. With his encouragement she examined the box, noting that it seemed to be an expensive, mahogany jewelry box. Opening it and finding nothing, she paused for a long time before making an observation. "I see a box that appears to be empty. I think it might have something in it, but I can't see anything. Perhaps you could help me."

Her friend smiled at the astute observations of his guest. Retrieving two packages from his wall cabinet, he handed them to the young woman. The first contained a replica of the box. The second was a large leather envelope filled with four smaller envelopes. She opened each one in turn and read the instructions out loud. After she finished reading, she agreed to follow the directive to visit each location soon.

When her host put the old mariner's compass in the center of the table, the young woman smiled at the thought. "I know I need a lot of direction, perhaps there is a clue in all that you've given me to show how this compass will help me get back on course and stay there."

"Perhaps there is," the older man added. Then he carefully reviewed her assignments. As he concluded, he added, "You've done very well tonight. You've already begun to see the meaning in each of the gifts. As you continue to study the gifts, you will gain some significant insights. With all the pressures you are facing, I think it will be a wonderful blessing."

Standing up from his chair, the host led his guest to from the study to the front door. After a brief conversation about her parents, he told her that they should meet again when she completed her assignments. He reminded her that he was available by phone whenever she wanted to call. He added that she should write her thoughts and feelings in a journal as the process moved along.

As she walked away from the house, she was pleased with the sense of direction and feelings of comfort she was carrying home. She was surprised to note that in a little more than an hour, the storm seemed to have blown over, though the air was still cold enough to make her pull the collar of her coat up around her neck. It was not until she got into the car that she remembered a fifth shelf in the crystal cabinet. She tried to remember the object on that shelf, but nothing came back to her. "I'll just have to let my curiosity rest for a while," she decided.

Over the coming weeks, she studied the objects whenever she had time, which was not as often as she would have chosen. The pressures of a single parent of three children working full time consumed nearly every minute. If it were not for her father, she would have taken much longer to complete her assignments. He immediately seemed to sense the importance of the tasks at hand and frequently made himself available for baby-sitting. The phone calls to her mentor helped move things along as well. Still, she worked late many evenings thinking and writing until finally she felt she was ready to talk face to face with her guide.

When she arrived at his home, the older man was pleased to see her enthusiasm for all she was learning. During a relatively short discussion, she demonstrated a reasonable understanding of the meaning of each of the gifts. They both agreed that there was still much to discover, nevertheless, he thought her progress was remarkable.

Before he had a chance to continue, the young woman's curiosity overflowed and she asked, "I can't wait any longer. What's on the fifth shelf?"

Her friend, visibly impressed with her skills of observation, answered, "That's something I added many years ago. It seems to be especially helpful for people in our day, in this age of hustle and bustle."

Walking to the étagère, he opened it and lifted the fifth object from its place. After placing it on the table between them, he said, "Please pick it up and tell me what you see."

She was silent as she picked up the object. It could be held in one hand. She turned it over slowly, examining it carefully with both hands before she studied the face. She looked slowly at each feature of the very old kitchen timer. There was nothing exotic about it. It was a simple, one-hour timer. It had originally been white, but had yellowed a little over the years. While the other gifts seemed to be of an ancient origin and of exquisite quality, the timer looked inexpensive, like something that could be purchased in a local hardware or discount store. She turned the handle and watched it move steadily back to where it had begun. A soft bell rang. She smiled, remembering a similar timer on the back of her mother's stove.

Finishing her examination, she said, "I see a classic kitchen timer. By classic, I mean it's a garden-variety timer. You could find a similar one in any mall or hardware store. And though it's typically used in the kitchen, I don't think that's the purpose here. That's what I see now."

The older man smiled as if he were remembering something, then quickly returned to the present. "This is my personal contribution to the more expensive gifts that you have been studying. I first saw it working in my mother's kitchen a long time ago. Under its influence, I ate some excellent meals. Occasionally, my mom would use it to teach other lessons. Tonight, I want to use it to help you discover some principles that have the power to change your life."

Taking a writing pad from his desk drawer and placing it on a clipboard, he handed it to the young woman along with a ballpoint pen. "When I start the timer, I want you to make a list of the most important events on your calendar during the coming week. You have five minutes to make the list. I'll give you an additional five minutes to prioritize the events in order of importance. Explain the importance. Please be honest and don't try to impress me."

When the bell rang, the young woman had listed twenty events on the first sheet. Then she prioritized them, attempting to be brutally honest. The first three items on her prioritized list were:

1. **My part of the annual report is due to management by Friday. This is vital to my annual review. A late report won't play well with my boss.**

2. **It's Mom and Dad's forty-eighth anniversary Saturday. We sent out forty invitations to the Open House. I'm the hostess. Everyone's counting on me to deliver a great activity.**

3. **The car needs work. It's been acting funny lately. I can't afford a breakdown this week. I have a repair appointment Wednesday morning.**

These two were further down the list:

8. **Randy (my fourteen year old) has a math test on Thursday. It's a midterm and he's been failing math. This one is critical. I'm pretty good at math and he needs help. I hope I can find the time.**

15. **Kathleen (my sixteen-year-old, emerging rebel) wants me to take her shopping for the prom in two weeks. With my schedule, I really don't have time. I'm not sure if this is my priority or hers.**

With only a quiet nod, her host picked up the timer again. "Now I want you to make another list. This time I want you to make a list of the people who are the most important to you. Then prioritize them. List at least fifteen people. Identify your relationship with each. You have five minutes for this activity."

The following is a sampling from her list:

1. **Three-way tie. My kids. Kathleen, Randy and Colin.**

4. **Two-way tie. Mom and Dad.**

6. **My sister Beth in Orlando.**

7. **Annie, my best friend not related to me.**

11. **My boss, Fred.**

13. **Three-way tie. Karen, Ralph and Carmen, all a critical part of my work team.**

While she was writing, her host took the four original gifts from the étagère and arranged them on the table between them. When she finished, she handed the list to her host. "Interesting," he said. "Now take your prioritized list and write by each name the average number of minutes you have spent in one-on-one conversation with each of these people this past week. It must be a personal conversation and in a calm voice."

A sample of her list looked like this:

Kathleen	8 minutes
Randy	4 minutes
Colin	15 minutes
Mom	2 ½ hours
Dad	45 minutes
Beth, sister	0
Annie, best friend	0

Fred, my boss	12 minutes
Karen, work team	2 hours
Ralph, work team	15 minutes
Carmen, work team	3 ½ hours

When she finished these activities, her host didn't say anything, but waited. The young woman turned the pages slowly, not really attempting to understand the result; rather she was searching for a solution. At first she was a little defensive as she tried to explain what was happening. Her host immediately diffused the issue. "In my experience, anyone who does these exercises ends up in about the same place. They realize that the people who matter most in their lives are being held hostage by people and events that matter less. The underlying question everyone has is what to do about it."

"Do you have a suggestion as to what I should do?" she asked hopefully. "I've been so busy trying to survive."

"Actually, I have several suggestions," he answered quickly. "But first I have some questions for you. I want you to look at the four other gifts and tell me what element of each gift applies to your situation. That is, where can a solution be found?"

Looking at the hourglass, she responded thoughtfully. "I thought a lot about my kids when I studied the hourglass. In fact, I think I said something about them when we looked at the hourglass the first night I was here. I know they need to be brought more directly into the present, but it's so hard with all I have to do."

"That's understandable. So where are you putting those who matter most?"

"Why they're conveniently stored in the future, so they won't bother me until later." She winced at the irony of her statement. "So what can I do to bring them more into the present?"

"That's a good question, and one I think you're going to have to answer yourself," he answered. "But I do have some suggestions that might help. Let's continue. Look at the mirror. What does it tell you about the issues we've raised tonight?"

She picked up the mirror, turned it over and read the message, "'What you see is not all of me.' I have been working to understand the differences between the heart, mind, and body. I've also thought a lot about the times when all three parts seem to be working together. Such times produce powerful, almost magical, results. I know my children need all of me. My heart, my mind, and my body. They've only been getting parts of each and not nearly often enough. It seems like I save the worst of me for them. However, if I had to choose one part from the mirror as the focus for the discussion we've been having, it has to be the body. The body is where action takes place. It's time to act and do it now."

"You're on the right track with those thoughts. Now let's look at the box."

Taking the box from the table, she opened it and once again felt the rich felt interior. "It's certainly not empty. Nor were the places you sent me." Then reviewing her lists, she came to a profound discovery. It turned out to be one of the critical moments of the evening. She waited for a long time before she finally found the words to express her feelings. "I need to say this out loud and see if it makes sense. When the Creator filled my space of life with others, His creations, and myself, I believe He intended us to give time to all three. I think the key for me is to find time for self-renewal, spiritual renewal, and time for my kids. When I do that, all the rest will fall into place. So how do I do it consistently?"

"The answer is in the simple kitchen timer," he responded helpfully.

"What am I missing?" She asked while picking up the timer.

"Sometimes the best learning happens when the right questions are asked," he answered. "Let me try some. What's the limit of the timer?"

"An hour. So how does that relate?"

"How much time would you need to spend with each of your children every day to make a difference?"

"Oh, at *least* an hour. But I can't do that. There are three of them, and I work. The weekends are full of catching up. How could I ever spend an hour every day in one-on-one conversation with each one?"

"Then what *are* you willing to spend with each child every day? One minute?"

"That's not nearly enough, as you put it, to even begin to make a difference in their lives." Then frustrated by what was happening, she changed the subject. "This conversation isn't fair. I can't do what I want to do, and I can't do what I need to do. I didn't make the choice for my husband to die, he just did. And I got left with all the work."

Not wanting to let the conversation stay there, the teacher picked up the timer and said in his most congenial tone. "On this timer are a myriad of choices. They range from one minute to sixty minutes. Look at its face. Tell me which number from one to sixty you could invest in each of your children every day. Choose something that you're willing to commit to."

The host's voice had a calming effect on the young woman. She took the timer from him and looked carefully at its face. "I think you've done this before. Do you have a suggestion?"

"Yes, I do," he responded cautiously. "Could you commit to spend five minutes every day in a one-on-one, calm conversation with each of your children?"

Because she knew this was a real commitment, she was unwilling to make it carelessly. She took a deep breath, thought about the meaning of her promise, and said, "I'll do it."

"Good for you."

As he was gathering up the gifts, he reached into the wall cabinet and got a white, garden-variety, sixty-minute kitchen timer. "This is my gift to you as a reminder of your commitment."

"Thank you," she responded, considering the task ahead. "I think I may need more than a timer. But I'm confident I can do this. I only hope it will work. It all seems too simple."

"My experience has taught me that it will work wonders," he answered confidently. Sometimes you may find you need more time, but if you do it every day in normal, calm tones, one-on-one, putting everything else aside, you'll be surprised at how fast the changes will come."

"Do you have any thoughts about topics?"

"Well, yes I do," he answered thoughtfully. "What's the most important thing you can tell a child?

"I think I should tell them that I love them," she said.

"Good idea."

"They'll think I'm strange."

"You are," he answered with a smile, "but they love you, so they'll accept you anyway. But you must also tell them why you love them. Give them specific reasons. You should be watching for things they do or say that you really appreciate and then tell them about it. And it must be honest and sincere."

As she was leaving, her host shared with her a story of his own first attempts at utilizing the principle of spending five minutes every day with those you love the most. She laughed at his description and decided to try it herself.

It was late when she got home. Her dad, who'd been babysitting, was asleep on the couch. Everyone else had gone to bed. She was relieved she had another day before the experiment began.

The next day was Saturday and provided ample opportunity for experimentation. She decided to try her mentor's approach with her easiest subject. That would be her younger son. Waiting until just the right moment, she walked up to him, put her arms around him and gave him a strong hug. "Colin, I love you more than words can say." And she waited.

Colin hugged her back and then retreated a couple of steps. "Mom, are you going to die?"

"Why no Colin," she answered. "I'm not going to die. Why would you ask that?"

"Well, last night, Grandpa and I were watching this TV program. The Dad found out he had cancer and was going to die. He went around hugging everyone and telling them he loved them. Are you sure you aren't going to die?"

"Yes, Colin," she answered emphatically, "I'm sure I'm not going to die."

"Okay, okay, I believe you." Then throwing his arms around her, he hugged her again. "I love you too, Mom." With that he ran upstairs to his room, leaving her behind with the feelings of success resonating inside.

"Well, it wasn't much," she thought. "In fact, it wasn't even five minutes, but it was a start."

Throughout the day, she found the opportunity to spend time with each of the other children. When she called her mentor that evening she reported that she had fairly good results. Her daughter cried before their twenty-five-minute conversation was over, and her older son promised to mow the lawn that afternoon even though she hadn't asked. She knew she had much to do to build the trust she wanted, but this was a beginning.

As her mentor finished his day, he wrote a closing note in his journal.

It's been a good day. One more person has used The Five-Minute Rule and is off to a good start because it's made a difference. Her success once again demonstrates that The Five-Minute Rule is an essential application of the gifts. I remember how apprehensive I was when I first added the timer and The Five-Minute Rule to the gifts. But each time I teach this, and someone applies it in their life, it makes a profound difference. It's also fun to teach The Rule to others. I love the timer. I think I enjoy the memories it brings as much as I do the principles that can be taught with it. And I love remembering beating the snot out of Freddie Martino that day.

After relishing the memory for another moment or two, he made a short entry.

I continue to feel the pain the doctor predicted. I guess my time is coming. Who'd have thought it when I was slapping the tetherball around? The real question is, who is my successor? I better get that taken care of soon.

EPILOGUE

13

The Successor

The story you have just finished is mine. I am the narrator. You have read a selected group of my "moments of learning." I am the young man whose life was changed by the miracle of the gifts. I was the one who came to the home of a teacher many years ago on a cold and dreary night, seeking answers. I learned much from applying the principles of the gifts. Later I was chosen to be the successor. For many years, I have shared these truths with countless others. I hope I have made a difference. Others will have to judge.

Some have asked if I ever learned the answers to my own questions. Others have told me I am much different than I was before I met the teacher. Truly, I was a reckless young man. In the years since then, I have learned that a life of service to others is the only way to resolve problems such as mine. Those who serve are twice blessed. As a man of wisdom wrote centuries ago, that which we do is restored to us. To the kind, kindness is restored. To the merciful, mercy is restored. To the just, justice is restored, and so forth. I have found these things to be true.

According to the ancient story of the gifts, at the close of the life of each teacher, he or she must choose a qualified person to receive the gifts and continue teaching the principles to those in need. As you know, I currently possess the gifts. I was told by the one who gave me the gifts that no one should ever know of the origin of the gifts except my successor. I am now in the twilight of my life, and it is my responsibility to choose the successor. This task has troubled me for many, many years.

When my mentor gave me the gifts at our last meeting, he included a leather-bound journal. Inside were precious, personal treasures—the writings of prior successors. Many had included valuable moments of learning from their lives. Others wrote words of encouragement to those who would follow them. I have been comforted by their thoughts.

For the past century or so, there has been common theme in the journal entries of the successors. It is a troubling problem, one that has worried me, too. I am including some of their thoughts here.

[The year is 1630.] *For forty years I have been honored to be the keeper of the gifts. Many have come to me, seeking my advice. The truth found in the gifts has guided them well. I now pass the gifts to another.*

[The year is 1752.] *In my days, no woman would expect to be chosen for such a job as this. But I, a common woman, was chosen to serve. God has blessed me in my efforts. Those who have come to me as seekers have found meaning in the gifts and their lives have improved. It is time for another to have this privilege.*

[The year is 1818.] *Our society is in upheaval. I have given away my life teaching the principles and sharing the wisdom of the gifts. It is not enough. There is more to do than one can finish. In the past season, seventy people came to me seeking my assistance. What is a woman to do? I have my own family to guide. My neighbors need me. Seventy seekers in a single year? It is impossible to meet their needs.*

[The year is 1854.] *We leave today for America. The gifts will come with me. There is no counsel in the notes saying I cannot remove them from my homeland. So I will take them. But who will guide the true seekers among my countrymen? Not me any longer. My life has been in peril every day for more than ten years. I long for a means to share the gifts with all. But I am only one man, what can I do?*

[The year is 1917.] *My son leaves today for the war in Europe. He is the second in our family to go. Thousands have gone before them. Who will teach these young men the principles and share the gifts? Many of them will not return. Countless homes will have an empty spot at their hearthside. What about all the families who grieve? The message of the gifts would give comfort and peace to all. But it is impossible for one woman to find them.*

[The year is 1931.] *The country is in turmoil. Families are in financial peril throughout the land and the number increases every day. Without work, families suffer. The President gives encouragement, but there is only so much the government can do. The principles of the gifts would help others find peace. I am an ordinary man and cannot meet such a challenge alone.*

[The year is 1942.] *Again the country is at war. Our enemy threatens invasion. I continue to be frustrated by my limitations. I can meet with only a few. The numbers who seek me out are overwhelming. The process of learning is slow, and there is only one who can teach. Is this wisdom? Perhaps, but surely there is a better way.*

[The year is 1973.] *Traditional values are being abandoned. Family ties are weakening. The principles of the gifts need to be more widely taught. I have considered selecting additional teachers, but when I visit the meadow, I feel constrained. Perhaps there will be a better time.*

And now, here am I, at the close of my life, pondering the future of the gifts. For more than one hundred years, the teachers have wished for help. Times have changed. Never have positive values been threatened as they are today.

We are in a new day in the history of the gifts and I think I have found a way to share the gifts with many more people. I have written the story of these ancient treasures to be widely circulated for the first time. It is my belief that more than one teacher must be chosen. All who read my story have been selected as keepers of the message. You have read the story. The gifts have selected you.

As you begin your role as a successor, there are certain requirements. First you must apply the principles of the gifts in your own life. When you have done so, you are authorized to teach others. I am including in these writings a brief summary of the instructions I was given when I was chosen to receive the gifts. There is much more to learn about the gifts, but this is a good start. On the last page, you will find my addition to gifts, The Five-Minute Rule.

I remind you that on each of the following pages are simple principles that encompass the wisdom of hundreds of years. As you read these pages, you will become possessor of the gifts. Use them wisely and well. To do so is to find happiness.

The Hourglass—Time

Meaning:

- The hourglass represents the three dimensions of time: Past, Present, and Future.

- The place where grains of sand cross from the future to the past is the "present moment." The present moment is the focal point of all activity.

- The past must be used as a resource and not be an obstacle. Be careful which grains you select from your past to contemplate and to use as a source for moments of learning.

- The grains of sand in your past are made up of your choices. Your behavior determines what collects in the bottom of your hourglass.

- Your future is created by what you do in the present. As each grain of sand enters your 'present moment,' it represents your opportunities and is molded by your behavior.

Application:

- Carefully search your past for important moments of learning. Write or ponder them, searching for their meaning. As you gain this skill, you will be able to find them in the present as they occur and you will be able to be a strong influence on the moments of learning in your future.

Your observations and commitments:

I.

II.

The Mirror—Self

Meaning:

- "What you see is not all of me."

- Your heart, your mind, and your body encompass all of you.

- Your heart consists of your emotions, feelings, creativity, and….

- Your mind consists of your thoughts, logic, reasoning, and….

- Your body consists of your actions, is the repository of your experiences, and….

- When you are at your best, you engage all of you—your heart, your mind, *and* your body. To do so is both possible and essential.

Application:

- Decide to choose happiness and other positive emotions.

- Seek balance within your heart, mind, and body.

- Strive to engage "all of you" when appropriate, especially in significant relationships.

Your observations and commitments:

I.

II.

The Box—Space

Meaning:
- The Creator filled the space of life with you, others, and His creations.

Application:
- You must give attention to all that is in your space of life.

- Serve others. They have been placed in your space of life so that you may learn to serve. As you do so, they will benefit. That's the most important part. But you greatly enhance your development when you serve selflessly.

- Accept service. Others have been placed in your space of life so that you may learn to be served by them. To be served is a blessing to you and to them.

- You must take time for self-renewal. You should develop the form of your self-renewal according to your needs.

- Take time for spiritual renewal. The exact form of your spiritual renewal is a partnership between you and your God.

Your observations and commitments:
I.

II.

The Compass—Guidance

Meaning:

- The compass represents guidance available to you as you seek truth. Some understand this guidance to be of spiritual origin; others see it as intuition or something wholly internal. For both, it leads them along the path of virtue.

- The feelings of Serenity and Peace that come when you are among God's creations or in other words, out in nature, are part of a larger guidance system that is represented by the compass.

- For some, guidance comes as a still, small voice that can be with them at all times. The compass may remind you of the still, small voice.

- The compass also represents the "knowing" that comes from contemplation of the divine. This knowledge can also come from seeking the possibility of something greater in life.

Application:

- Let the symbol of the compass remind you to seek truth and virtue.

- Use the principles related to the compass to find a balance between understanding your impressions and acting upon them.

Your observations and commitments:

I.

II.

Kitchen Timer—The Five-Minute Rule

Meaning:
- The Kitchen Timer is the symbol for **The Five-Minute Rule**. The timer reminds you that if you can do something for one minute, you can do it for five.

- Properly applied, **The Five-Minute Rule** is a point where the dimensions of life—time, self, and space—meet.

Application:
- Spend at least five minutes alone every day with those you love the most, either in person or by phone. At that time, tell them you love them. To be most effective, you must give them specific reasons why you love them. The power of The Five-Minute Rule is in telling them why.

- Spend at least five minutes every day one-on-one with others who mean the most to you: coworkers, friends, & extended family. Tell them you appreciate them. Again, the power is in telling them why.

- Embrace spiritual renewal. Seek peace in your daily walk. Spend five minutes every day with your God.

- Practice self-renewal. Spend at least five minutes every day with yourself.

- **The Five-Minute Rule** works best when practiced consistently over an extended period of time. **Do It Now!** Don't wait to start using **The Rule**.

Your observations and commitments:
I.

II.

Tell us about your success using the Five-Minute Rule,
So that we may share them with others.
Visit us at www.TheFive-MinuteRule.com

About the Authors

Rory J. Aplanalp has impacted the lives of more than one million people across the globe. Known for his energy and ability to make people laugh, Rory's high impact presentations are interspersed with humor, personal anecdotes and practical wisdom. Rory's client list includes ExxonMobile, Chase Bank, BMC Software, PriceWaterhouse Coopers, REMAX, AT&T, MPI, Hearst Publishing, SHRM, Nestles, General Motors, US Department of Justice, MD Anderson Cancer Center and Verizon. Originally from Salt Lake City, UT, Rory resides in Houston, TX, and enjoys spending time with his wife Cindy and their eight children. He believes that his greatest success is being able to have a lasting, positive effect on others.

Donald P. Mangum has spent 25 years teaching and speaking to leaders and individual team members, guiding them through a wide-variety of organizational, team, and group challenges. Don has a gift for helping others simplify complex issues and assisting them in reducing those issues to manageable, bite-size pieces. Don's clients have included Ford Motor, US Steel, Xerox, Monsanto, Pfizer, JM Huber, Federal National Mortgage Association, Oliver Products, Abbott Laboratories, Dow Brands, Libby Owens Ford, Lincoln Laboratories, The Bank of Montreal, Volvo and Bell Canada. Don is co-creator of the *Authentic Leadership Workshop and* is the author of three books on personal development and human relations. The father of seven children, Don and his wife Diane currently reside in Houston, TX.

Contact Information: For more information about Rory and Don's broad range of services, including speaking, consulting, training, and published materials (books, training workbooks, cassettes, and videos), please visit the website at: www.rory.com or email us at rory@rory.com or dmangum1@aol.com. Toll free number: 877-817-7679.